FR. GABRIELE AMORTH

FR. GABRIELE AMORTH
Rome's Exorcist

THE OFFICIAL BIOGRAPHY

DOMENICO AGASSO

TRANSLATED BY BRET THOMAN, OFS
FOREWORD BY FR. CHAD RIPPERGER

TAN BOOKS
GASTONIA, NORTH CAROLINA

Translated by Bret Thoman, OFS

Cover design by David Ferris—www.davidferrisdesign.com.

Cover image: Father Gabriele Amorth, The Vatican's Chief Exorcist - Rome, Italy - 04 Oct 2010. Image contributor Vandeville Eric/ABACA/Shutterstock. Used with permission.

ISBN: 978-1-5051-3158-1
Kindle ISBN: 978-1-5051-3159-8
ePUB ISBN: 978-1-5051-3160-4

Published in the United States by
TAN Books
PO Box 269
Gastonia, NC 28053
www.TANBooks.com

Printed in the United States of America

"And the seventy-two returned with joy, saying: Lord, the devils also are subject to us in thy name. And he said to them: I saw Satan like lightning falling from heaven. Behold, I have given you power to tread upon serpents and scorpions, and upon all the power of the enemy: and nothing shall hurt you. But yet rejoice not in this, that spirits are subject unto you; but rejoice in this, that your names are written in heaven."

—Luke 10:17–20

CONTENTS

PUBLISHER'S NOTE

TAN Books has been at the forefront of fighting the battle against the devil. From manuals on spiritual warfare, books on the saints, the Church's enemies, prayer, virtue, angels, heaven, purgatory, hell, the devil, and so much more, TAN Books seeks to equip you with the spiritual ammo to conquer sin and so defeat the devil. For the surest way to overcome the devil is by becoming a saint.

It is TAN Books' great honor to offer the official biography of Father Gabriele Amorth in English for the first time, a translation of Edizioni San Paolo's Italian version, *Don Amorth Continua, La biografia ufficiale*. The author gives a list of selected books he used to write this biography in the bibliography. In these pages, you will learn about Fr. Gabriele Amorth, the most renowned exorcist of the twentieth century, and how he became an exorcist. Even more importantly, you will discover a saintly soul, a priest who walked among saints, a priest who labored until his final breaths for the salvation of souls.

Father Amorth spent sixty-nine years in the Pauline order, which published the Italian version, so it is fitting that they publish his official biography. May Fr. Gabriele Amorth's extraordinary yet humble life inspire you in your battle against the devil, the flesh, and the world. May you follow his example of prayer and deep devotion to Our Lady.

The Publisher

FOREWORD

Many exorcists in the last twenty years have viewed Father Gabriele Amorth as a father of modern-day exorcism. This can also be said of Father Candido, but Father Amorth was the one that communicated the knowledge and wisdom of past generations of exorcists into the modern era. As this biography shows, his writings in this area provided and still provide an initial look into the realm of the spiritual battle. The *Rituale Romanum* of 1962 is still often the ritual used today by many exorcists, used by Father Amorth for a majority of his exorcisms. However, the second paragraph of chapter one of Title XII states, "In order to exercise his ministry rightly, he should resort to a great deal more study of the matter (which has to be passed over here for the sake of brevity), by examining approved authors and cases from experience." Father Amorth is generally considered to be one of those approved authors today. Due to the accessibility of the writings in translation in English, he has become one of the main authors

studied by priests who recently and currently are training to be exorcists. Father Amorth is known for explicat-
ing sound practice in exorcisms. There are many approved
authors scattered throughout the history of the Church, but
Father Amorth, in his short books, provided many sound
principles and practices for the exorcist to keep in mind;
in that sense, we can consider him an "approved" author.
Yet, Father Amorth also provided training for priests who
would go to Rome and attend sessions he conducted over
the possessed, providing a valuable formation to future
exorcists. His continued writing and work in this area, following in the footsteps of Father Candido, bridged the gap
between the pre-conciliar years and the decades after the
council in the area of exorcism, which had seen a drastic
decline in the Church's practice of exorcism. This bridging
of the gap would prove essential for the resurgence of the
work of exorcism, at least in the United States. In so many
ways, Father Amorth can truly be said to be a father, if not
the father, of modern exorcism.

His life started with a normal childhood, which is an
important quality in an exorcist for the sake of his psychological development. Exorcism is a battle, often waged in a
person's interior life, and so a normal childhood provides
a psychological balance to the exorcist. Father Amorth was
also grounded in solid work as a priest before becoming an
exorcist. The rituals normally state that bishops should not
pick a priest to do solemn exorcisms unless he is "properly
distinguished for his piety, prudence, and integrity of life"
(*Rituale Romanum*, Title XII, ch. 1, no. 1). Under normal
circumstances, this will be observed in his priestly life and
work over the course of years. It is time as serving as a priest
which makes it possible to observe if he is prudent, pious,
and has integrity. These three qualities, when possessed by

a priest, reveal his being grounded in his priesthood, which is key, since demonic attacks can be destabilizing to the priest if he is not well grounded. He will be one who has a clear identity as a priest, one who sacrifices regularly, can fast regularly, and is known as a man of consistent prayer. He will be seen as one who has no human respect and has a singular vision for God. Father Amorth is a good example in this regard, especially being known as a man of prayer.

He had a sense of his own nothingness, as the reader will discover in the coming pages. This is the hallmark of a good exorcist: to truly know that one is a useless instrument, as Christ tells us (see Lk 17:10). Any exorcist who is honest and who has done exorcisms even for a short period of time realizes that no demon obeys him, except insofar as he is obeying Christ. Without Christ, the priest can do nothing to compel a demon to anything. This humility was clearly demonstrated in the life and words of Father Amorth.

He was known for his sense of humor, and humor among exorcists is a necessary quality for many reasons, but above all for the reason of being able to strike a good balance in their view of themselves and of their work. The best exorcists are those who are serious in session, but can also be light hearted outside of session. There are times in session when the demons will do or say something that is very humorous, but the good exorcist can maintain a seriousness despite this diversionary tactic. Yet, not having a sense of humor can be a sign of being overly serious or taking oneself too seriously, which is dangerous in this line of work.

His devotion to the Blessed Virgin Mary is demonstrated throughout his life. In fact, one would doubt that Father Amorth would be able to view his work in any other way than through the lens of Our Lady. Priests that do exorcisms for years, and in some cases decades of their priesthood, know that this work is impossible without her intervention. She is, after all, the one that crushes Satan's head, and any exorcist who has done exorcisms for any length of time can recount stories of Our Lady's involvement in their work. Father Amorth was clearly no exception. He is a great example to the power of Our Lady's protection throughout the years of his work. In many cases, of which Father Amorth is likely one of them, it is really Our Lady who chooses them to do this work. This is evident by signal graces in the priest's life and manifests itself in his devotion to her. Clearly, the consecration of Father Amorth's family to the Blessed Virgin during the time of war is an example of a signal grace. Our Lady's predilection and choice of him to serve in this role is even signaled by the demons themselves, who recount that he is protected by her.

If it is true that she chose him, it is even more clear in his life that he did not chose to be an exorcist. A good exorcist normally is not one who chooses this apostolate. Father Amorth seems almost flabbergasted that he was chosen to engage in the spiritual battle in a way and intensity that most others do not. However, once assigned, he dedicated himself to it. One of the reasons one could surmise that Our Lady chose him was due to his connection to publications. He made the work, and the necessity for it, known.

As the founder of the International Association of Exorcists, he provided a forum for the formation of priests in the area of spiritual warfare as well as an organization where exorcists can be in contact with each other for the sake of consultation. Some have questioned the number of exorcisms he did. By some estimates, it is between forty and seventy thousand. It sounds impossible, but it is not as unimaginable as one might think. The average time to do the solemn rite of exorcism, from start to finish, is between twenty-five and thirty minutes, provided one does not stop to repeat a specific line that afflicts the demons during the session. When one hears forty to seventy thousand exorcisms, we are obviously not talking about the number of people, but the number of times that the priest recites the ritual. As Father Amorth points out, it often takes numerous sessions or exorcisms with the same individual, sometimes over the course of years, in order to liberate the individual. So it is entirely possible, in fact, one may say, it would be surprising if he had done exorcisms almost full time for thirty some years and not have done that many.

Father Amorth laments and suffered through a very common experience of virtually all exorcists: that is the dual battle of those who do not believe in Satan and the battle with Satan itself. This is by no means a recent phenomenon. Even Blessed Francisco Palau, who was an exorcist and a peritus at the First Vatican Council, gave Saint Mary Anthony Claret a few harsh words over the idea expressed by Saint Mary Anthony that diabolic problems are really just psychological problems. Obviously, many people who come to an exorcist suffer from psychological problems, but occurrences that are clearly preternatural can be explained in any adequate why by recourse to psychological analysis. Father Amorth suffered this dual battle, as the battle against Satan is a call to sacrifice, a call to prayer and fasting, to suffering attacks both upon one's person and in one's externals. But the second aspect of the dual battle is truly dealing with clergy and bishops who do not think Satan is real, who would prefer to think that Satan does not exist, because if he does, then the life of even the average priest shifts significantly. If a priest or bishop can convince himself that

Satan does not exist, that the faithful should not engage the battle even in their own lives, or that he as a priest or bishop has no real obligations to aid those in spiritual need who are under attack, then he can preserve his comfortable priesthood and life. While many bishops do believe and do engage in the battle, so few do. Part of this battle that an exorcist must endure is to come to knowledge of a case in a bishop's diocese, and yet, the bishop refuses to help or even hear about the case. Sometimes the bishops do not help out of simple incredulity, as one bishop once said to an exorcist, "I believe in the devil, just not in my diocese." Or in another instance, a bishop told an exorcist, "I have never given faculties for this in the twelve years I have been a bishop." The exorcist had to bite his tongue and not retort with the obvious response, "Well, your excellence, that is not a virtue." One of the most consoling and encouraging experiences an exorcist can witness is when the bishop himself does the exorcism, even if it is only a minor exorcism. One of the sufferings an exorcist must endure is knowing how powerful the fullness of the priesthood is in spiritual warfare and how few bishops truly engage in it. All of these things, Father Amorth bore in his lifetime.

Father Amorth's death is like many great figures in history, who despite having a human side, their passing left a sense of loss to us on this side. No doubt he is interceding, even for exorcists and the afflicted, as this is an ongoing battle, and so he is, in one sense, more powerful now through his intercession than perhaps he was even in this life. But all we can do is await for God to raise up other great men, who will gird the battle armor left for us by Christ, so that His presence in their strength, virtue, and knowledge is still seen to be with us. In the meantime, Father Amorth has left us a great patrimony in his writings to which exorcists now and in the future can look as one of the "approved" authors. For those who knew Father Amorth, they can truly see in his life the Scripture passage: "I have fought a good fight; I have finished my course; I have kept the faith. As to the rest, there is laid up for me a crown of justice which the Lord the just judge will render to me in that day; and not only to me, but to them also that love his coming" (2 Tm 4:7–8). And one last passage, "For, when he hath been proved, he shall receive the crown of life which God hath promised to them that love him" (Jas 1:12). May Father Amorth intercede for all of the diabolically afflicted and for all exorcists.

Fr. Chad Ripperger, PhD

INTRODUCTION

THE NAME OF EVIL

"Cast out demons!" Jesus commanded the disciples in the Gospel. He personally confronted the devil for forty days in the desert. He resisted. He fought. He was victorious. Not even hunger could wear him down: "Turn these stones into bread," Satan said as he tried time and again, tirelessly. What a victory it would have been to have triumphed over God Himself, incarnate in His Son Jesus. But Jesus did not give in to the persuasive tempter.

Though he was unsuccessful in the temptation of Jesus in the desert, the devil certainly did not give up. He continues—"forever and ever"—to test every person in the world. This is why he exists. His task, his "mission," is to take away as many souls as possible from God, to snatch creatures away from their creator. How many people today, however, still believe in the existence of the devil, or in his works and victories? This is perhaps his greatest feat: convincing the world that he does not exist, that he has disappeared forever. Instead, he operates subtly, striking defenseless creatures. They are defenseless because they are incredulous: What is there to defend against if evil no longer exists? In fact, the tempter has succeeded in convincing us all—or almost all of us—of his non-existence. He slinks down, hides, and negates himself in order to strike better, conquer, and enlarge his dominion all the more. He has managed to convince the many that he is little more than a fairy tale—like the big, bad wolf and the bogeyman used to get children to behave.

Perhaps worse, the Church herself seems to have forgotten the devil. After having focused on him for centuries, now, and with modernity run amok, she has abandoned the challenge. It is as if the Gospel did not exist, in its warning, insisting, and repeating again and again that the heart of every man—even of Peter and of Judas, two of the twelve closest to Jesus—can be conquered by the lord of evil. Scripture attests to the fact that anyone can be overcome, with disastrous results both to the individual and the whole of humanity. No. It seems that not even the Gospel is sufficient anymore—nor the many saints, popes, bishops, and priests who have all stood up to the evil one for over two thousand years.

We have eliminated the devil, sin, and ultimately death, as unpleasant, anachronistic, out-of-date themes. Dismissed as the stuff the Middle Ages, modern man no longer has time for such ancient nonsense. Instead, there are other far more exciting and thrilling challenges that inspire modern man. The concepts of good and evil themselves, moreover, have changed in today's mentality. What is good and what is evil? Who can say? Everything is relative. Everyone has the right to construct for himself one's own tailor-made sense of good and evil. And if doing so harms others, what does it matter? Is man free or not? Can man do what he wants with his life on earth or not? Indeed, humanity is rushing toward a dark and frightening end— one we have already seen and experienced before—namely, *homo homini lupus* (a man is a wolf to another man).

It should be enough to have eyes to see. Is it not demonic that practically half the world is at war? Or that there are prisoners, refugees, the hungry and thirsty, the persecuted, and the tortured? Or that unspeakable violence is being inflicted against children, women, and the elderly? Is it not satanic that little ones are being killed in the womb, as are the sick who have no hope? Or that hatred breaks up families, that racism poisons souls, or that ideologies run rampant within individuals and nations?

"The smoke of Satan has entered the Church," said Pope Saint Paul VI in the 1970s. That same smoke seems to have enveloped the entire world, intoxicated consciences, disordered minds, and destroyed human coexistence. Good resists, of course, and continues to resist. It often defeats and repels the formidable assaults of evil in its thousand forms. But what is at the root of evil? The action of the devil, now and forever. Pretending that he does not exist will not save us from his bullying, insistent, and pervasive actions. Therefore, taking the Gospel seriously, believing in Jesus Christ who died and descended to the dead and rose again, means becoming aware that evil has a name and a face: that of the devil. He is an unwelcome presence, of course, but real and tangible, forever and ever.

Fortunately, there are men in the Church who are willing to look directly at Satan, confront him, fight, and overcome him. They are the exorcists. They are priests who are meticulously trained for this terrible task. Their work requires taking on the prince of this world and driving him out as written in the Gospels, as Jesus commands. Often unknown or little known, sometimes misunderstood or even derided, exorcists are a powerful weapon against the spread of the evil one, his conquest of hearts, and the victory of evil over good.

The following pages recount the human and spiritual ventures of the most famous exorcist of our era, Fr. Gabriele Amorth. For thirty long years, he carried out this crucial role with total dedication as long as his strength permitted. Not only did he go to war against the devil, he taught others to do so. He spoke and wrote about his ministry and involved countless people in his work. He spent his life urging Christians—including priests and even bishops—to believe in the existence and pervasiveness of the devil. He illustrated the modern manifestations of evil in all its forms—often captivating and striking.

Encouraged by the last three popes—Saint John Paul II, Benedict XVI, and Francis—he fought the good fight, kept the faith, and finished the race. He was a relentless enemy of the prince of this world, and he defended the cause of Jesus and His Church—at the same time one, holy, catholic, and apostolic, and also imperfect and sinful. If others are now fighting on that difficult battle front, it is certainly due to him. He restored visibility and nobility to the ancient practice of exorcism, drew young priests into the battle, raised awareness among the bishops, stood at the side of the faithful, and put us all on guard against the temptation to eliminate the devil. Anything less would grant the devil the highest victory: believing that he does not exist, letting down one's guard, and becoming estranged from God and the Church—from faith, hope, and charity.

1

TWO SAINTLY PARENTS

Gabriele Amorth was born in Modena (in Emilia Romagna, Northern Italy) on May 1, 1925. The government of Italy had been Fascist for almost three years. Benito Mussolini was then a young man from Forlì, a city in the same region. Previously a socialist, he took power without bloodshed on October 28, 1922 in the infamous march on Rome. It was not a triumphal march, but it was enough to convince both King Victor Emanuel III, the government led by Luigi Facta, Parliament, and the Italian people of the inevitability of change.

The postwar period was marked by protests, clashes, and violence between the reds and the blacks.[1] Order was needed, and the sanguine man from Romagna appeared as

---

[1]   Colors denote political ideologies and can vary from region to region. The Italian political landscape cannot be reduced to a two-party system, such as the "red states" and "blue states'" of American political parlance. The struggle for identity referenced here was between fascism (denoted as "blacks" from the color of the fascist uniforms) and socialism (the "reds," or Soviet communism).

the savior of the homeland. All of Italy appeared ready to genuflect before Mussolini, to prostrate themselves, and to place themselves at his beck and call. As history unfolded, however, this was a monumental mistake of extraordinary import that would be paid for with tears, bloodshed, and ruin. In 1925, Fascism became victorious and the country was transformed into a dictatorship, bringing an end to the constitutional, liberal, and parliamentary state. On January 3, Mussolini gave a dramatic speech to Parliament where, subsequently, political parties and unions were suppressed, and newspapers were censored. The head of government became master of the country under the impotent—and partially complicit—gaze of the king of Italy. The Italians, with some culpability, entrusted the destiny of their country to one man, Mussolini.

Fascism, however, had no place in the Amorth family. Gabriele's father Mario was a lawyer and co-founder of Father Luigi Sturzo's *Partito Popolare* (Popular Party, or the People's Party) in 1919. The party appealed to the "free and strong" and called Catholics to action and political witness.[2] This movement arose long after the capture of Rome in 1870, which had marked an end to the temporal power of the papacy. The former archbishop of Milan, Cardinal Achille Ratti, was now seated on the chair of Saint Peter as Pope Pius XI. Times were changing, and the unification of Italy was an accepted historical fact.

The carnage of the First World War (1914 to 1918) drew warnings, prayers, and pleading for peace from two popes. Pius X prophetically foresaw the warning signs of the future "Great War," and Benedict XV used forceful words against

---

[2]   The Popular Party was comprised of Roman Catholics who opposed communism.

"the useless massacre." The tragic and violent postwar period prompted the Sicilian Fr. Luigi Sturzo and Mario Amorth to mobilize Catholics. The *Partito Popolare* called Italy's Catholics to resistance so as to prevent the country from spiraling into an endless struggle between the new working class and entrenched nobility. Unfortunately, however, Father Sturzo's *Partito Popolare* was not successful. It was swept away, along with others, by the winds of fascism.

Nonetheless, the "people" of the People's Party and its Catholic ethos were not swept away–the lawyer, Mario Amorth, being among them. The son of a lawyer himself, Gabriele's father was born in 1884. His wife, Albertina Tosi, two years his younger, was very active in the local parish. They had five sons: Leopoldo, a future lawyer who followed in the footsteps of his father and grandfather; Giovanni, a doctor; Luigi, a teacher; Giorgio, a magistrate; and finally, Gabriele, born in 1925.

Not much is known about Gabriele's childhood and adolescence. Gabriele recounted simply, "I was born in Modena on May 1, 1925, into a very religious family. My parents were two saints. My four brothers (we were five boys) were all truly golden. We were very close." Paolo Rodari offered a glimpse into Gabriele's childhood which he recounts in his book *L'ultimo esorcista* (The Last Exorcist):

As a child, I used to go to Mass with my mamma and papà in Modena, where I was born. I often fell asleep on the floor, under the pews, at my parents' feet. When I slept and remained silent without running back and forth through the aisles of the church, my mom would reward me, usually with a piece of candy. If, on the other hand, I was agitated and noisy, I got no reward. For me, these things were good and evil.

They were my whims and my mom's smiles, the jokes
and caresses of my father, and tears and consolations.[3]

Gabriele reports that he wanted to become a priest at a
young age. The faith and zeal that animated the Amorth
household certainly nurtured his vocation: daily attendance at Mass with his mother, the holiness of his parents,
and the goodness of his brothers.

The call came early. As Gabriele recounts, "I attended
classical [high] school and, already at the age of thirteen, I
began to think about the future, about the priesthood, and
about religious life." He adds, "I have always been accustomed to obeying. The idea of becoming a priest came to
me when I was twelve years old. It was 1937. In obedience
to God's call, I considered it. I never felt drawn to other
paths. Although I always had cordial relations with girls, I
felt inclined to the priesthood. I had my crushes, but always
left them there. In fact, this was useful to me. Due to this,
I made a real choice between marriage and priesthood,
and not a theoretical one."[4] Gabriele recounts that he had
a normal, lively, and carefree childhood, with no apparent
mysterious signs about the future. Catholicism and the
sacramental life were central in the Amorth home, something which would bear fruit much later. He states, "I had
a clearer perception of evil when I confessed the first time.
Then I understood that evil is serious and we must strive
to correct ourselves. I was taught to confess weekly."[5] His
vocation was precocious, no doubt.

Gabriele wanted to be a priest but also had a normal childhood. He was involved in athletics, excelling

3   Amorth, *L'Ultimo Esorcista*, 16.
4   Amorth, 12.
5   Amorth, 16.

particularly in fencing and cycling. He demonstrated extraordinary skills of discipline, commitment, and seriousness, and was spiritually mature compared to others his age. He participated in Catholic Action and in the San Vincenzo Association in his parish, attended catechism, and even won a trip to Rome in 1936.[6] He also served as diocesan president of Catholic Action youth and was later appointed group leader and deputy delegate of the aspirants. He exercised leadership from a very young age. He did well at the Muratori classical high school he attended in Modena, and graduated in 1943.

In the meantime, however, Fascism and Benito Mussolini were advancing in the worst possible ways. Allying himself with Hitler, *il Duce* (Mussolini) took Italy to war on June 10, 1940. Gabriele Amorth was only fifteen years old. The new terrifying carnage, even worse than the first war, would bloody the world for five terrible years. From 1940 to 1945, death, mourning, hunger, and despair ravaged Italy. World War II destroyed people and projects, cities and families, dreams and hopes. Even the church of San Vicenzo was struck by a bomb in 1944.

The war devastated the lives of millions of people. How deeply the war affected the young Gabriele is unknown, but the spiral of human violence and the extermination of millions of Jews in the Nazi concentration camps was a genocide of unimaginable proportions. For those who lived at that time, this was hell on earth. The truly demonic underpinnings of the

---

[6]   Catholic Action sought to imbue Catholic values into the broader, secular (and often anti-clerical) culture at the time. Devotion to San Vincenzo is common in Modena, where Father Amorth was raised. Saint Vincent was part of the Theban Legion who refused to offer sacrifices to the emperor and were consequently martyred (circa AD 286).

war became increasingly obvious in the abyss of cruelty and despair that has few precedents in the history of humanity.

The evils of war and political corruption form a backdrop for young Gabriele Amorth, who continued his studies without putting aside his goal of religious life. In the summer of 1942, with the war still raging, Gabriele was beginning his final year of high school. He went to Rome with his parish priest. As he told Paolo Rodari, "I felt inclined to community life, to life in some religious order."[7] Because he was fond of several Passionist priests from his region, he specifically sought information about the Passionist Order. He wanted to enter a congregation but had no specific preference, as he did not yet have any direct knowledge of the orders.

That trip to Rome changed the course of his life. It was a decisive encounter, the first of many. The Passionists had no rooms available to offer Gabriele and his parish priest, but they were directed to Father Giacomo Alberione and his newly formed Order of St. Paul. Though the Paulines had no rooms there either, they permitted the pair to sleep in the infirmary. There, Gabriele Amorth met Father Alberione for the first time. Of short stature from the region of Piemonte, Father Alberione founded the Pauline Order with the mission of proclaiming the Gospel through modern media. That encounter would prove decisive for the future of the young Gabriele.

Gabriele confided in Father Alberione, known as the "apostle of the good press," of his desire to become a priest. As Saverio Gaeta recounts,

> I heard [Alberione] speak then for the first time. He
> was saying things that made me believe I was in the

---

[7]   Amorth, *L'Ultimo Esorcista*, 12.

presence of a man of God. Thinking he could help me resolve my questions, I asked him to pray for me and ask the Lord what I should do. He promised me that the following morning he would celebrate Holy Mass for me. I showed up to serve (at 4:30 in the morning!). I figured that by seeing me present, he would remember me. After Mass, I went to talk to him and he limited himself to a single sentence: "Enter St. Paul's." Without delay I was satisfied, and I truly accepted that answer as coming from the Lord.[8]

The following year, 1943, Father Alberione was passing through Modena and was hosted by the parish priest of San Pietro. Gabriele was aware of the founder's plan to build a large sanctuary in Rome dedicated to Our Lady, as a gift of thanksgiving for Mary's intercessory prayer for saving the lives of all Paulines scattered throughout the world during the war. Father Amorth later said:

In my family, we were five brothers, all military age. I asked the First Master [Ita: *Primo Maestro*, that is, Fr. Alberione] to extend this vow to my family, as well.

8   Gaeta, *L'eredità segreta di don Amorth*, 9–10. He described his encounter with journalist and writer Elisabetta Fezzi in *La mia battaglia con Dio contro Satana* (My Battle with God Against Satan): "At seventeen, in my second year of high school, I met Don Giacomo Alberione, the founder of the Pauline Family, who gave me the final nudge. I asked him: 'So, what does the Lord want from me?' I wanted God to tell me what to do. Instead, thanks to [Alberione], I understood that it was up to me to decide. All the same, God intervened and Don Alberione told me: 'I will celebrate Mass for you tomorrow morning.' After Mass, he communicated to me: 'That you enter into [the Society of] St. Paul!' 'Okay,' I replied. But I was in second [year of high school], so I proposed:'"I will finish my third year and then enter.' Fezzi, *La Mia Battaglia Contro Satana*, 16.

He accepted, assuring my mother as well, who knew nothing about my intentions for the future. All five of us experienced things, but we came out of the conflict safe and sound. My mother kept repeating until her death that we were saved thanks to that intercession, and she always sent offerings of thanksgiving to the Queen of Apostles sanctuary (built in Via Alessandro Severo in Rome as a fulfillment of that vow).[9]

This encounter would weigh decisively in Gabriele Amorth's choice of religious life.

Here are found the early seeds of Gabriele's devotion to the Blessed Mother and the power of Marian consecration. As Father Amorth recalls:

I was aware of the fact that Don Alberione had consecrated his spiritual children to the Queen of Apostles with a vow so that Our Lady would protect them all. I did so too. I asked Don Alberione to consecrate me and all my family members to the Queen of the Apostles. The war started, and the war ended. And, like all my brothers, I was not injured. Not one bullet ever touched me or my brothers. Despite enduring terrible dangers, we all came out unscathed. This meant a lot to me. Until just before I was ordained, I still had a doubt in my mind not so much about priestly ordination itself as about the place where God wanted me to become a priest. I wondered, "Am I really doing the right thing by entering the Paulines? Is this really where God wants me? Or does he want me somewhere else?" My doubts were removed on the day of

---

[9]   Gaeta, *L'eredità segreta di don Amorth*, 10–11.

my ordination. My mother greeted Don Alberione and said to him, "Thanks to the consecration you made to Our Lady, my Gabriele and his brothers were saved. I cried for joy." With that simple statement, my mother confirmed to me that Our Lady had protected me thanks to the consecration of Don Alberione, and that she wanted me in the Paulines. Our Lady saved me from death during the war so that I would become a priest. And I became a priest with the Paulines.[10]

Henceforth, the close relationship with the Virgin Mary became the cornerstones of Gabriele Amorth's entire life. That distant personal consecration to the Mother of Jesus would accompany him forever. He once quipped, "Why do today's mothers not consecrate their children to Our Lady too? It doesn't take much: a simple prayer made by a priest with this intention. All children should be consecrated to the Immaculate Heart of Our Lady. They would enjoy unique protection." That simple gesture of consecration, for Father Amorth, "means erecting an invisible but impenetrable protective shield around the person."[11] This impenetrable and protective shield will accompany him for the remainder of his priestly life.

---

[10]   Amorth, *L'Ultimo Esorcista*, 24–25.
[11]   Amorth, 25.

2

"ALBERTO" THE PARTISAN

As the war drew to a close, chaos ensued in Italy. On July 25, 1943, the Grand Council of Fascism dismissed Mussolini, who had led the country to the precipice of a humiliating defeat. After the king had him arrested, however, Mussolini was freed by the Germans and sought refuge in the North and founded the Social Republic, also known as the Republic of Salò. Salò is named after the Lombard city on Lake Garda where Mussolini and his last faithful leaders had taken refuge and had barricaded themselves in. He called his young followers to arms, but they instead hid or fled to the mountains.

On September 8 that same year, the armistice of Italy was signed. Finally—after the English and American Allies landed in the South, the Italian army was demobilized, and the king himself fled from Rome to Brindisi. What would be known as "the Resistance" was born as many young people became Partisans, and they organized to fight against the Germans and Fascists for the liberation of Italy in collaboration with the Allies. Traces of a desire to resist against evil are seen here in the life of Gabriele Amorth. As Gabriele recounted:

> There was the war. I didn't want to abandon my brothers and my family during that period, so I told Don Alberione: "First, I will enroll in the university [and later enter the congregation]." "Very well," he replied. [So] I enrolled in jurisprudence and fought in the war. I received a military medal of valor for my role fighting for the Partisans on the mountains and plains around Modena. Then I joined the Christian Democrat [the political party that formed after the Popular Party of Gabriele's father], because the new Constitution was about to be conceived. We were all in agreement in saying, "Now we must commit ourselves to the Constitution; afterwards, everyone can do as they wish."[12]

With that, he postponed entering the Pauline Order. Notably, he had first wanted to make his contribution as a Christian to the liberation and rebirth of his country.

In the spring of 1943, a few months before the dismissal of Mussolini and the armistice, a group of young Catholics met secretly to chart a course different from the bleak present. Among them was Gabriele, just eighteen years old and (still) desiring to become a priest. Notably, Gabriele Amorth gave his unconditional support to the cause. He joined forces with many men who would later become important for the direction of Italy and the Church. Giuseppe Dossetti, a university assistant and a leading Partisan in Emilia

---

[12]   Fezzi, *La Mia Battaglia Contro Satana*, 16.

Romagna (the region of northern Italy with Bologna as capital). Dosetti later became a politician and cofounded the Christian Democrats. Venerable Giuseppe Lazzati was also there. Venerable Lazzati would later, at the request of (then) Cardinal Giovanni Battista Montini (archbishop of Milan and future Pope Paul VI), become editor of the Catholic newspaper *L'Italia* and the rector of Catholic University. Amintore Fanfani was there too. He had a storied political career, later serving as a deputy and senator, minister and secretary of the Christian Democrats, prime minister, and president of the Senate.

From September 1943 to April 1945, however, Italy was a battlefield. There were Partisans and Allies on one side, Nazis and Fascists from Salò on the other. It was a bloodbath. Not only were soldiers dying—inevitable in every war—but countless innocent civilians were victims of Nazi-Fascist thugs, Allied bombings, and Partisan excesses. It would not be easy to rebuild the country so full of hatred, resentment, a desire for revenge, and violence, not to mention the material and spiritual ruin that invested it.

Catholics would need to commit themselves to reconstruction. In the front row was the Christian Democrat Party—the "daughter" of Father Sturzo's Popular Party—led by Alcide De Gasperi. Many young men who participated in the Resistance came together: Dossetti, Gorrieri, and Fanfani. Then there were Moro, La Pira, Mattei, Marcora, Taviani, and others. The "best Catholic youth" were leaders during this extraordinary season of rebirth and renewal of Italy and they collaborated with the other protagonists of the struggle for liberation: communists, socialists, liberals, unionists, and monarchists. Together with soldiers, priests, and men and women, they made a vital contribution in those terrible days during and after the war.

There are few specific episodes to narrate regarding
Gabriele and the Resistance. It is known that Amorth chose
the *nom de guerre* "Alberto" and fought in the Partisan unit
made up of Catholics known as the *Brigata Italia* (Italy
Brigade), led by Ermanno Gorrieri, who used the *nom de
guerre* Claudio.[13] In autumn of 1943, Gorrieri began organizing clandestine meetings in the parish church of San
Pietro. Together with Dossetti, they discussed the future of
Italy and placed their hopes in a handful of generous and
courageous young Catholics. Though they were not fully
aware of the dangers and difficulties that lay before them,
their desire to see their country free of Fascism and its Nazi
occupiers was such that they could overcome, or at least
minimize, their fear. Dosetti, who later became a priest
and was present at the Second Vatican Council, said of the
future exorcist's influence on this group of young Catholic
resistance fighters, that Gabriele "guaranteed, so to speak,
orthodoxy of thought."[14]

The contribution of Gabriele and his band of Catholic Resistance fighters helped to shape the future of Italy.
A common misconception held by the media and biased
historians is that, in the postwar period and for a long time
thereafter, reconstruction was carried out almost exclusively by left-wing Partisan units, especially Communists.

---

[13]   Gorrieri was another eminent figure within Italian Catholicism.
Born in 1920, from Sassuolo, he was one of the promoters of the Partisan Republic of Montefiorino, in the mountains between Modena and
Reggio Emilia, and one of the founders of the "white" CISL union. He
was a Christian Democrat deputy, minister, and finally, in 1993 (with
Pierre Carniti), the creator of the Social Christian [party]. Having
broken away from the Christian Democrats, they did not go over to
the new Popular Party of Mino Martinazzoli, who joined the Leftwing
Democrats—that is, the former Communist Party.

[14]   Gaeta, *L'eredità segreta di don Amorth*, 6.

This is not the case. Gabriele and his coreligionists and fellow Resistance fighters were key to holding off both fascism and communism in Italy. The man who would later single-handedly resist the devil in single combat showed his grit in these formative days before his priesthood. As Gabriele recounted, "A first meeting was held in Modena. It was organized by Ermanno (Gorrieri, who took the *nom de guerre* Claudio) but headed by Gianfranco Ferrari, and held in the rooms of Catholic Action (next to the prison cells). Flyers were distributed, and young people were encouraged not to become Little Republicans (*repubblichini*), that is, Fascists. They rather [should] go to the mountains."

"To mountains" meant joining the Catholic resistance. He recalls how he worked with "Claudio" in "organizing groups of Partisans and to bring food and clothing supplies back up to those in the mountains." The young Gabriele was fearless in the face of danger. He recalls how "Claudio" and "Alberto" escaped capture and execution: "One evening, by the Formigine cemetery, we were captured by two Fascist soldiers. We knew well that if we had been led away by them, we would have been killed. We managed to escape through the fields covered with snow, disguised as two Little Republicans, and we continued to fight."[15]

For the young man between eighteen and twenty who desired to be a priest, his participation in the Resistance was anything other than symbolic. Saverio Gaeta lists Gabriele's leadership roles within the Resistance: "Unit commander with 40 men corresponding to Second Lieutenant (5 November, 1943 - 10 March, 1944), unit commander with 105 men corresponding to Lieutenant (11 March, 1944 - 20 November, 1944), unit commissioner

---

15   In Gaeta, *L'eredità segreta di don Amorth*, 7.

with 225 men corresponding to Captain (21 November, 1944 - 31 December, 1944), unit commissioner with 560 men corresponding to Captain (1 January, 1945 - 30 May, 1945)." He also received commendations for bravery. Gaeta reports that Amorth received "the war cross for Partisan activity, with the subsequent enrollment in the Blue Ribbon Institute among fighters decorated with military valor."[16]

At long last, on April 25, 1945, after the Second World War finally ended with Mussolini's execution by the Partisans, the conception of the initial government headed by the parties that had led the Resistance came to fruition. Gabriele could have entered politics as did many of his fellow Partisans. In fact, as Gabriele himself recounted, "At the age of twenty-one, in 1946, I was appointed national deputy delegate by the then president of the Christian Democrat Youth: Giulio Andreotti himself."[17] Alberto the Partisan was going "to the mountains" again, but this time for a higher cause. Leaving a promising political career behind him, he set his sights on his true mission and battleground, the priesthood.

---

[16]   Gaeta, *L'eredità segreta di don Amorth*, 7–8.
[17]   Amorth, *L'Ultimo Esorcista*, 17.

3

AN AGREEMENT WITH FATHER ALBERIONE

abríele Amorth was cut out to be a politician. His Partisan qualifications, leadership skills, and charisma meant many possibilities for an intelligent young man like him. As noted above, several of his peers went on to have long careers in the new Italy. Initially, Gabriele Amorth collaborated in the preparation of the Constituent Assembly that led to the new Constitution, voted on June 2, 1946. At the same time, there was a referendum which chose a republic as the new form of government and led to the exile of the final king of Italy, Umberto II.

Gabriele, however, was not quite finished with politics. The way he recounts it, it sounds simple. In reality, the postwar period was quite complicated. After his experience with the Partisans, Gabriele returned to school, pursuing a law degree in the steps of his father. He joined FUCI, the Italian Catholic Federation of University Students. At that time, it was led by a young monsignor from Brescia, Giovanni Battista Montini, the future Pope Paul VI. Two

other men, who eventually had storied careers in politics
(Aldo Moro and Giulio Andreotti) also helped. As Gaeta,
who was present as a delegate at the national congresses of
the organization, said:

> [Amorth] participated for a brief period in the initial
> stages of the Christian Democrats. Already during
> the clandestine period, he had launched groups in
> different areas in lower Modena. He was the first to
> be elected as a student representative at the University
> of Modena, and he was appointed provincial delegate
> to the Christian Democrat Youth. In this capacity, he
> was present in Assisi for the first national meeting of
> youth groups of the Christian Democrats, with his
> subsequent appointment as National Deputy Dele-
> gate from the end of 1946 to the first half of 1947. The
> national delegate was Giulio Andreotti, who on June
> 1, 1947 became undersecretary to the prime minister.
> The Christian Democrat leadership asked Amorth to
> take over his role in leadership for the youth, but by
> now his religious vocation had definitively matured,
> and he declined.[18]

It was not as if Gabriele had determined that politics
was not for him as much as he knew that the priesthood
was for him. He had made the choice at the age of thirteen
and he never changed his mind. He had an "agreement"
with God, and one with Father Alberione. He recounted:

> At the time, I was a member of the political group
> of Giorgio La Pira, Giuseppe Dossetti, Amintore

---

18   Gaeta, *L'eredità segreta di don Amorth*, 8–9.

Fanfani, and Giuseppe Lazzati. When Andreotti was promoted to the undersecretary of the prime minister, they suggested I take his place. But I didn't consider it for one moment. I got out of politics, and I sought my place among the most faithful of God. I went to Don Alberione and became a Pauline. I was ordained a priest in 1954. From 1954 until 1986, for thirty-two years, I was a simple Pauline priest with positions at various levels of leadership within the society.[19]

Alcide De Gasperi, the prime minister of Italy, called the young Andreotti, then twenty-eight years old, to serve alongside him. Gabriele Amorth then witnessed remarkable opportunities in politics open up before him. He could have risen to the highest ranks in the government. But he chose differently—perhaps disappointing some and surprising others. How is it that he refused such opportunities? To some, it made no sense and was humanly incomprehensible and inexplicable. But not for him. He told Elisabetta Fezzi:

> I belonged to a group led by Giuseppe Dossetti, my professor of canon law at the University of Modena. He taught at Cattolica and commuted between Milan, Modena, and Reggio Emilia. Fanfani, Lazzati, and La Pira belonged to this group, all men of great esteem. After the promulgation of the Constitution, everyone went his own way: Fanfani remained in politics, Dossetti was held back by Cardinal Lercaro who suggested (wrongly) that he run as candidate for

---

[19]   Amorth, *L'Ultimo Esorcista*, 17.

the municipal elections of Bologna. Then he became a religious and founded a very strict congregation of both men and women. Lazzati went to Catholic University, and I became national deputy delegate of the Christian Democrat Youth, a vicar to Andreotti. When Andreotti entered the government, he stepped down from the Christian Democrat Youth, and I sensed that they would nominate me to take his place. Then I, too, resigned. I realized that if I had continued in politics, I would never have gotten out. Instead, I wanted to be faithful to my pact with Don Alberione. So I withdrew. I graduated [with a degree] in jurisprudence in four years and immediately entered [the Society of] St. Paul. I did my novitiate in Alba, then theology in Rome, and on January 24, 1954, I was ordained a priest. It was the centenary of the dogma of the Immaculate Conception, and they delayed my first Mass so we could celebrate during the Marian year.[20]

Gabriele graduated in 1946 with a thesis titled *Rosmini and the State Constitution*. Such a choice was by no means accidental. His work represented his deep concern for the future of Italy. His religious vocation, however, was stronger. In this, he never wavered, not even during the darkest days of the war. His vocation was now making itself felt again and was pushing him toward something higher and greater than "partiality"—that is, political "partisanship." His calling was service to God and His Church, a universal mission addressed to all people in the world.

---

[20]   Fezzi, *La Mia Battaglia Contro Satana*, 17.

Leaving the secular world behind, he then went to Alba, the small capital city in lower Piemonte. This was the heart of the spirituality of Fr. Giacomo Alberione and homeland of the Paulines. There, Gabriele would receive a new mission, to be a Pauline priest. These modern apostles of the Gospel sought to bring the Word of God to every corner of the world with the tools of modern communications: books, newspapers, cinema, and television to the internet and social media of today.

Perhaps it was Father Alberione's simplicity and stability which drew Amorth to the Paulines. Unassuming and of small-stature, Father Alberione was born in 1884 in San Lorenzo di Fossano. Like Gabriele, Giacomo Alberione's vocation came at an early age, and he entered the diocesan seminary of Alba, where he studied philosophy and theology. On New Year's Eve, December 31, 1900—the night straddling two centuries—while praying in the cathedral, among the *Te Deum* of thanksgiving, Mass and communion, and Eucharistic Adoration, the young Alberione found his vocation. There were no particular revelations or enlightenment; that is, he did not hear a voice, have a vision, or experience some other divine sign. Again, like Amorth, there was an inner awareness, a vague inspiration. It was more like a warning that he needed to prepare himself to do something important—a prodding that would never abandon the sixteen-year-old boy from the countryside. Alberione wrote many years later that he "felt obligated to serve the Church, the men of his era and to do so with others."[21]

There, on that night between the nineteenth and twentieth centuries, the Paulines were conceived—not

---

[21]   Agasso, *Don Alberione Editore per Dio*, 18.

immediately, of course. Indeed, as is the experience of many founders, Father Alberione would experience difficulties and struggles in the conception of his new congregation. But the seed was sown, which, in the following years and decades, would bear abundant fruit. His extraordinary intuition was that of creating a new religious family whose mission was that of proclaiming the Gospel through social communication. His congregation would utilize new vehicles of communication to bring the Good News to the people where they were. In this way, he could reach even those who did not go to church. Following the example of Saint Paul the Apostle, he would strive to bring the Gospel to the whole world. Gabriele was drawn both to this man and to this mission.

Fr. Silvio Sassi, the late superior general of the Paulines, wrote, "Fascinated by the personality of Saint Paul, Father Alberione actualized the mission of the Apostle of the Gentiles." Father Sassi cites Archbishop Ketteler (then archbishop of Mainz), who said of Father Alberione: "If Saint Paul returned today, he would become a journalist," and I firmly believe it. Saint Paul lives again in the 'Apostolate of the Press.'"[22] Thus seeing himself in the footsteps of the apostle, Alberione saw the necessity to create new and modern ways of proclaiming the Eternal Word. He notes:

> Since it was not a question of creating a simple Catholic publishing house in the Church, but a *society of apostles* dedicated to full-time evangelization, Don Alberione abandoned the initial idea of forming an organization of Catholic laity to instead found a religious congregation in which the members would be

---

[22] Agasso, 11.

engaged in personal sanctification and in the missionary work of publishing. Since *oral preaching* is entrusted by the Church to the priest, *written preaching* should be done by the priest-writer. As in the parish, the priest has collaborators, the priest-writer needs collaborators to be able to carry out the apostolate of the press, which includes editing, running the press, and getting the media out to the public. A strong organization is needed: this is the Pauline *parish*.[23]

Such was the Lord's vineyard entrusted to Giacomo Alberione, the son of farmers, and to his followers and successors.

The Pauline beginnings were certainly not easy. Alberione's was a new and unprecedented ministry, one which would prompt fear, uncharitable criticism, and renunciation. There were rumors that a rather revolutionary priest was out there stealing vocations from dioceses and looking for money to build his "cathedral" of printing presses, paper, and ink. But the temperament of the man—who appeared slight and fragile—had been formed among pious farmers from the Piemonte region. These men of the soil kept their heads down, spoke few words, and were accustomed to hard toil.

As Father Sassi recounts, "The apostolate of the press is the specific charism of the priest-writer of the Society of St. Paul . . . assisted by consecrated laypersons (Disciples of the *Divin Maestro*) and by the Daughters of St. Paul (founded June 15, 1915). Pauline nuns and consecrated laypersons, grafted onto the consecration of Pauline priests, acquire a quasi-priesthood status, because,

---

[23]   Agasso, 11.

making it possible in all three aspects of the apostolate of the press, they contribute to the supernatural efficacy of Pauline publishing." [24]

This charism is what drew Gabriele. From Alba, the presence of men and women devoted to the proclamation of the Gospel would radiate throughout the world with the widespread publication of books and newspapers. Father Alberione wanted a Bible in every household, and he unleashed his followers with all the means of communication to bring one into homes at an affordable price. He founded a newspaper, *Famiglia Cristiana*, which would be handed down from generation to generation, reaching circulation in the millions. He opened bookstores. He would try his hand at cinema, radio, and television. He even had, moreover, the full support of Pope Paul VI.

The vision became a reality. Father Sassi explains the order's rapid growth:

> To guarantee the development of the apostolate, to allow the formation of young Paulines and the consolidation of the necessary structures, the association of men and women lay collaborators was conceived (*Pauline Cooperators*, 30 June, 1917). Don Alberione's foundations also included the Sister Disciples of the Divine Master (10 February, 1924); the Sisters of Jesus Good Shepherd (*Pastorelle*, 7 October, 1938); the Sisters of Mary the Queen of Apostles (*Apostoline*, September 8, 1959). Then there are the secular Institutes: the Institute of Jesus Priest, the Institute of St. Gabriel the Archangel (*Gabriellini*), the Institute of Our Lady

---

[24]   Agasso, 11–12.

of the Annunciation (*Annunziatine*), and the Institute of the Holy Family (founded beginning in 1957 and approved on 8 April, 1960).

"All the Institutes," recalls Father Sassi, were "the express will of the founder, comprise the Pauline Family." This family, however, was not simply a Catholic printing business. They were first and foremost *Catholic*, and as such called to holiness. Every component of "ecclesial life in the apostolate of the press" should be imbued with "contemplation, collaboration with parish priests, direct contact with the people, the need for vocations, etc."

After a long and industrious life, Fr. Giacomo Alberione, the *Primo Maestro* of the Paulines, died in Rome at the Generalate on Via Alessandro Severo, 58. An hour earlier, Pope Paul VI knelt at his bedside. He was attended by one of his daughters, Sister Giuditta, who recalls his final moments: "'*Primo Maestro*, His Holiness is here,' said Sister Giuditta, who was assisting him. Her effort was in vain; he could no longer hear. The Pope (Paul VI) then knelt beside his bed, prayed, and gave him absolution in Latin. After a look around the small study where the dying man was lying, he wrote a message on a register: '*In nomine Domini, Paulus PP VI*, 26 November, 1971.'"

Thus, the Holy Father placed the seal of Peter on an extraordinary and unique life, which ended at 6:25 p.m., precisely one hour after that visit. Thirty-two years later, another pope, John Paul II, included the name of Giacomo Alberione among the ranks of the Blessed in Saint Peter's Square. Don Alberione's most significant contribution to the Church was as a pioneer of evangelization: Pauline activity has been declared an apostolate, alongside oral preaching, declared of high esteem before the Church and the world.[25] The prophet of social communications had reached his goal and the mission of the Pauline apostolate: personal sanctification. The small seed of one era had produced a giant tree, whose good fruits continue to spread in the Church. This was the man to whom Gabriele Amorth entrusted himself and his future.

---

[25]   Agasso, 13.

4

FROM POPE PIUS
TO POPE JOHN

Gabriele Amorth arrived in Alba in the fall of 1947 when he was twenty-two years old. Due to his years of study, service in the Resistance, and a brief foray into politics, he was now seasoned in the world. This world, however, he soon rejected. Six years later, on January 24, 1954, he was ordained a priest in Rome by the bishop of Norcia, Monsignor Ilario Roatta. Gaeta recalls the words of Father Alberione to the newly ordained Paulines, which included now Father Gabriele and fourteen companions: "Be ministers of truth in charity: may this truth form in you a hope yearning for the reward, and with consummate charity, so that your entire lives and energy are consumed for the Lord."[26]

Gabriele, known for his jesting, saw a playful pun in being "consumed for the Lord." He suggested that his brothers add a phrase to the invitations to his ordination: "The Amorth family, licking their chops, announces Gabriele's

---

[26]   Gaeta, *L'eredità segreta di don Amorth*, 11.

31

pretonzolato" [a term of endearment for priesthood, but also a word which means "pre-wrapped" like food]." His light-heartedness would serve him well in his later work as an exorcist.

Now Father Gabriele celebrated his first Mass in his home parish church of San Pietro in Modena, where he was baptized. In his first sermon, he spoke words which now seem prognostic in light of his years of work as the world's most renowned exorcist: "The priest is an announcer of joy and a nourisher of hope, because he reminds everyone that, after this world, there is another infinitely better one. It is true that his mission is beyond human abilities, but he must not be dismayed by this: to carry out his work, he is granted an overabundance of graces which will never fail him. Therefore, even a petty and unsuitable man, by the mere fact of being a priest, is equipped with a supernatural strength that allows him to accomplish exceptional things."[27] These traits reveal the secret to being a good exorcist: humility, simplicity, and recognizing that despite one's human weaknesses and deficiencies, the priest is filled with an abundance of graces to carry out his mission.

Father Amorth's mission began simply. At the age of twenty-nine, and newly ordained, his first assignment was in Alba. This was a natural fit for him to grow in the Pauline charism, as it was the cradle of spirituality for the sons and daughters of Father Alberione, the house where the First Master founded his family. There, he began his service in the "good press" of the Order of St. Paul. He soon became director of the small monthly publication *L'Aurora* [The Dawn]. He also taught in the congregation's

---

[27]   Gaeta, 11–12.

internal seminary, which was full in those years. He was a gifted teacher and spiritual master. He explained, "In the early days, I was in Alba as the spiritual director of a group of young people. I taught Italian in our high school and began writing articles for *Famiglia Cristiana* and other Saint Paul newspapers. I also began to preach retreats and spiritual exercises."

His time in Alba, however, was brief. In the spirit of Saint Paul, who went out to bring the Gospel to the nations, Father Alberione sent his people immediately "in the field." He would hear no hear excuses and echoed the command of Jesus: "The harvest is abundant but the laborers are few; so ask the master of the harvest to send out laborers for his harvest" (Mt 9:37–38). Father Gabriele would receive on-the-job training, as Father Alberione sent his "laborers" out—with no experience, with no money, and with little preparation—"into the harvest" around the world. Here, Father Amorth would put into practice the insights of his first homily: a priest trusts not in his own strength but in Jesus Christ. Just as Jesus sent forth the disciples "without a money bag or a sack or sandals" but lacked nothing (Lk 22:35), so Father Alberione sent his newly ordained priest. The Paulines certainly wore out their footwear. They went tirelessly to the farthest and strangest—and at times frightening—places. They always returned (seemingly) victorious, having brought the word of God everywhere and in union with the Great commissioning of Jesus to the apostles: "Go, therefore, and make disciples of all nations, baptizing them in the name of the Father, and of the Son, and of the Holy Spirit" (Mt 28:19).

While his confreres enjoyed apostolic success, Father Amorth struggled in his first years as a Pauline missionary.

The year 1958 was crucial for Fr. Gabriele Amorth. He said
to Elisabetta Fezzi:

> The year 1958 was a bit odd. Don Alberione told me
> to step down from the positions I had in Alba because
> I was needed in Bologna at [the newspaper] *Avvenire
> d'Italia.* Coincidentally, I was already a friend of the
> director, Raimondo Manzini, though Don Alberione
> was unaware of this. It seemed as if they were intend-
> ing to hand over the paper to the Society of St. Paul.
> Instead, the plan fizzled. Then, another one was
> born: Fr. Agostino Gemelli asked Don Alberione if
> he would free me up to go to Milan to become spiri-
> tual director for the university students at Cattolica.
> I accepted. But after a short time, Father Alberione
> told me: "Give up on that too, because you are needed
> for another assignment." But that one, too, fizzled. In
> short, everything went sour that year.

While doors seemed to be closing on the young priest,
he was being guided to another key pillar of his priesthood,
something which would accompany him into spiritual battles for the rest of his career: Marian consecration. As he
explained, "So I came to Rome to the publisher's office. I
was in Rome without a permanent position. I spent a little
time at the publishing office and some time outside. But
soon the most beautiful endeavor of my life would be conceived. That year, when I was essentially unemployed, I got
the idea. A brother who died in the air of sanctity, Don Stefano Lamera, had suggested it to me. He said, 'Consecrate
Italy to the Immaculate Heart of Mary.' The country had
never been consecrated, ever!"[28] Father Amorth had always

---

[28]   Fezzi, *La Mia Battaglia Contro Satana*, 18.

had a love for the Virgin Mary, and had worked in Marian newspapers and wrote about her in various books. Now, the idea of consecrating Italy to the Mother of God consumed him, and he threw himself into the project.

Change was in the air. In those days, Italy was still deeply Catholic, as demonstrated by the political elections of 1948. The Christian Democrats obtained an absolute majority, following a fiery electoral campaign against the socialist-communist bloc headed by Togliatti and Nenni. De Gasperi led the reconstruction as head of government until 1953, when he was ousted by figures in his own party. Among the leaders of the era was an old companion of Father Amorth, Amintore Fanfani, with whom he fought in the Resistance and helped organize the future of Italy.

There was also a change in the papacy. The 260th Vicar of Christ, Pope Pius XII (Cardinal Eugenio Pacelli had succeeded Pius XI on March 2, 1939) died on October 9, 1958 in Castelgandolfo. While his papal motto was *Opus iustitiae pax* (the work of justice [shall be] peace), his long pontificate of almost twenty years had included the tragic Second World War (1940–45).[29] In fact, he faced the most frightening war in all of history, one that left millions dead and Christian peoples fighting against Christian peoples. He was harshly (and unjustly) criticized for not doing enough to defend the Jewish people deported to Nazi concentration camps.[30] Despite the terrible years of the conflict, at the

---

[29] Hitler had even sought to imprison the pope. Pius XII had to prepare a plan to abdicate should the Germans enter the Vatican, leaving Cardinal Eugenio Pacelli, allowing the Church to elect a new successor to Peter.

[30] These "shadows" on his alleged silence have weighed on his path to sainthood, which has begun but not yet concluded. For an historical sketch of Pope Pius XII's work to help displaced Jews hide from the Nazi's, see Rabbi David G. Dalin's excellent work *The Myth of Hitler's*

pope's behest, bishops, priests, friars, and nuns did their utmost to help Jews. At great risk, they hid them in convents, churches, sacristies, and other religious houses and buildings. There were many acts of heroism on the part of men and women of the Church. Many, in fact, paid for their commitment to the persecuted and to the pacification of the country with their lives.

The fifty-one cardinals of the conclave elected Cardinal Angelo Giuseppe Roncalli, born in Sotto il Monte (near Bergamo). On October 28, 1958, one month before he turned seventy-seven, the new pope, then the patriarch of Venice, took the name Giovanni (John XXIII): "*Vocabor Johannes*" (I will be called John). He explained right away that he chose the name not only of the Baptist and the Evangelist but because it was his father's name. His motto was *Oboedientia et pax* (Obedience and peace). Born on November 25, 1881 into a large farming family, Pope John XXIII would lead the Church five short years until June 3, 1963. He would leave his mark and had a very clear plan. He convened the Ecumenical Second Vatican Council, which was concluded by Paul VI. After the stern years (amidst tumultuous times) of Pope Pius XII, the affable John XXXIII sought to show the world a paternal and pastoral face of the Church.

Italy had only recently been rebuilt. Though still led by the Christian Democrats, the country was changing from agricultural to industrial, with the inevitable advantages and disadvantages. There was talk (and action) of involving the left, at least the socialist part, within the government. In the meantime, little by little, almost imperceptibly, mores

---

Pope: How Pope Pius XII Rescued Jews from the Nazis (Regnery Publishing: Washington, DC, 2005).

were changing. The television helped unify Italy, but it was also changing the country—and not always for the better. The country was in ferment, and so was the Church. The arrival of Pope John's Second Vatican Council was just around the corner. And yet the world was not paying attention. In the Soviet Union, Khrushchev was entrenched in power. Though he had vigorously rejected the horrors of Stalinism, he continued promoting the errors of communism. In America, the presidency of the young Irish Catholic John Fitzgerald Kennedy was about to begin. The media, in fact, often grouped the three leaders together— Khrushchev-Kennedy-John XXIII—in speaking about the news and hopes for a future without war and without poverty, a new springtime for the world and for the Church.

In that fall of 1958, while the new pontiff was "becoming pope," the young priest Gabriele Amorth set out to consecrate Italy to Mary. It was a massive enterprise, one that would involve the entire country from north to south. It would go down in history as one of the moments of greatest exposure of the Catholic world in Italy that was showing initial signs of change—religious and cultural and, in particular, economic.

What exactly did consecration to the Virgin Mary mean? Would it be an anachronistic initiative? Or a useless "show of strength" by Catholics who felt that the world was passing them by? The world was experiencing new and unprecedented historical changes which seemed to relegate the Church to a more subordinate position with respect to the past. These risks and cultural tumult was not enough to cool the zeal of Father Amorth, or his organizational machine. Nor did it stop the enthusiasm of the promoters. Father Amorth, the seasoned politico, organizer, and decorated military officer who lead soldiers in combat as part of the Resistance, was up for the challenge. He stated:

> Because of *Avvenire*, I was friends with dear Cardinal Lercaro and I wrote to him [about the Consecration]. He thanked me for it, took it upon himself, and got it approved by the CEI [Italian Episcopal Conference]. What a success the Lord had! But I got it rolling: I wrote to Lercaro, who immediately accepted and submitted the project to the CEI, which then consisted of twenty-five members. But in the meantime, I had "catechized" almost all of them. And so, when there was a show of hands to approve the Consecration of Italy to the Immaculate Heart of Mary, there were more hands raised than those present. Many raised both hands! Lercaro did not know this, but I had already gone to the various bishops to prepare them for this unscheduled vote. Then he appointed me secretary of the organizing Committee and told me: "You do everything!" And so, in 1958 and 1959, I dedicated myself to the Consecration of Italy to the Immaculate Heart of Mary. The doors were all wide open, and all the bishops immediately approved the plan. There was precious little time to prepare.[31]

This singular and unprecedented undertaking marked a fundamental stage in the relationship of Father Amorth to Mary, the Mother of Jesus. He said to Paolo Rodari:

> My life has been marked by Our Lady. This manifested itself in a powerful way in 1959. On 13 September of

---

[31]   Fezzi, *La Mia Battaglia Contro Satana*, 18–19.

that year, Italy was consecrated to the Immaculate Heart of Mary. It took place in Catania as the culmination of the XVI National Eucharistic Congress. It was an admirable harmony between Eucharistic worship and the veneration of Mary. With that event, the nation wanted to remain with the Virgin for a reawakening of faith, greater frequency in ecclesial worship, and a new Christian commitment to society. Surprisingly, I was entrusted with the coordination of the entire event. Not only that, in the previous months, I also had to arrange to get the statue of Our Lady of Fatima to all the provincial capital cities. It was a year of hard work—a year dedicated to Our Lady, to the kingdom of light.[32]

Just what would take place? What does it mean, concretely, to consecrate Italy to Mary? It was completely new, and there were no precedents to reference. It had to be created from scratch. Father Amorth recounted:

There was a Jesuit, Father Mason, who suggested, "Get [the statue of] Our Lady of Fatima to come. She will preach for you. Have her come to all the provincial capital cities by helicopter." The helicopter was the only way to be fast. We got it thanks to the aid of Andreotti, who was constantly of help to me. So we prepared the calendar and all the bishops immediately approved it. Thus, on 25 April, 1959 we began in Naples, and by the end of the summer we had been to all the provincial capitals. The Consecration of Italy was undertaken in Catania at the end of the National

---

[32]   Amorth, *L'Ultimo Esorcista*, 25–26.

Eucharistic Congress, on 13 September. There were just a few months, and we had to go everywhere without considering if the day was a Sunday or a weekday . . . just one or two days in each city and then we were off.[33]

The statue came from Fatima, the Portuguese village where the Virgin Mary appeared to the little shepherds Lucia, Jacinta, and Francisco the first time on May 13, 1917. This massive undertaking would involve all the regions of Italy. Nonetheless, as the Virgin of Fatima arrived by helicopter to various towns and villages, she was welcomed everywhere by cheering, weeping crowds.

The Marian pilgrimage and formal Consecration of Italy by the bishops was an unforgettable chapter in the history of Christianity in Italy. Of course, not everyone appreciated the momentous event. There were non-believers, anti-clerics, and leftists alike who expressed opposition. They labeled it as a form of exasperated and anachronistic devotion and attacked it as a political initiative spearheaded by the Christian Democrats to get votes. This did not stop the Catholic faithful crowds who came out *en masse* for the public events around the statue of Mary.

Father Amorth arranged for at least two unplanned events for the Virgin Mary. One involved Padre Pio, the other Father Alberione. He recalled, "Since I was organizing the events and I had been a spiritual son of Padre Pio for some years, I reserved a day for Our Lady to go to him. I still remember that for some reason we had set aside two days in Benevento. So I wrote to the bishop of Benevento asking him to give up one day, and he accepted. Thus, I

---

[33]   Fezzi, *La Mia Battaglia Contro Satana*, 19.

used that day to send her to Padre Pio. Then, of course, I also had her land at the *Regina Apostolorum* for Don Alberione and the Paulines who were there."[34]

This would prove a personal success, too, for the young Pauline priest. He stated, "It was the most beautiful experience of my life. I really felt like a useless servant, useless and good for nothing, but an instrument in the hands of God: all the doors opened wide for this project! That is how the Consecration of Italy to the Immaculate Heart of Mary was made! It was a great project! A great event!"[35]

Wherever the Virgin Mary is, however, the enemy always seeks to thwart the graces she brings. Father Amorth admitted:

> However, after Our Lady passed, the doors closed. At first, it was a huge success everywhere, and I insisted to the bishops that we prepare a [post-pilgrimage] publication. But they always said no, that it wasn't necessary. Enough, they said. They didn't want to hear about it anymore. And when I tried to get things moving so as to publish a small booklet . . . I tried to do it, and it went badly. I should have let her arrange things! Then, yes, it would have been done. . . . If I had only let Our Lady act!"[36]

This lesson of "letting her arrange things" in the face of opposition would come to imbue his entire priesthood, including his work as an exorcist. The Resistance fighter would encounter resistance to true devotion both from without *and* within the Church. But he now was organizing

---

[34]   Fezzi, 19–20.
[35]   Fezzi, 20.
[36]   Fezzi, 20.

for a higher cause, and did so with his customary zeal. Father Amorth recounted:

> Later, I tried to celebrate the twenty-fifth anniversary [of the Consecration] in Trieste, but it was a failure. I had a direct rival there in the president of the CEI, the archbishop of Turin, Cardinal Ballestrero. He was very much in opposition, as he was staunchly against devotionalism. He said it was a form of devotion, and he rejected every proposal I made to the CEI. For this reason, there were no initiatives, and there was no anniversary. Instead, I wrote a booklet for preaching for the month of May. In those days, the month of May was still practiced in the parish churches. I wrote it to help the parish priests, and it sold like hot cakes. In fact, several editions were printed in a very short time.[37]

Henceforth, and often in the face of fierce opposition, all of his priestly endeavors would be marked by a Marian consecration which "let her act" in and through him.

---

37   Fezzi, 20–21.

5

OUR LADY'S TRAVEL BY HELICOPTER

ather Amorth detailed the great undertaking of the Consecration of Italy to Mary, an event that was monumental for the Italian Church and all those involved. The rapid changes experienced during the time period of the pontificates of Pius XII and Pope John XXIII were difficult for the Catholic Church in Italy. The tension between the difficult postwar period and monumental economic boom would transform the lives of countless Italians—politically, socially, culturally, economically, and morally. This meant, for Father Amorth, an even greater necessity for Our Lady's intercession.

Father Gabriele would later refer to the Consecration of Italy to Mary as "the most beautiful chapter of my priestly life," in which he felt he was an instrument of things greater than himself. He meticulously recounted the origin and development of the project:

> In early September 1958, Don Stefano Lamera, superior of the Roman house of the Pious Society

of St. Paul, called me out of the blue to entrust me
with a special task: "Go to Cardinal Lercaro and ask
him and the bishops to support the Consecration of
Italy to the Immaculate Heart of Mary. He will listen
to you, and it will happen." Previously, when Father
Lamera was director of [the monthly] *Vita Pastorale*,
he had published a letter with a similar request and
had the support of some bishops. There was immediate enthusiasm from four good, young men from
Verona who wrote urgently about this initiative and
encouraged him to become the spokesperson for it, as
there was an upcoming Eucharistic Congress in the
Diocese of Verona. I did not think that this invitation would ignite such a great fire. I was chosen based
on the fact that Cardinal Lercaro knew me. In that
period, my congregation, the Pious Society of St. Paul,
was considering taking over the newspaper *Avvenire
d'Italia*. For this reason, I had been to Bologna several
times. Working with the cardinal, I was delighted
to discover an old friend from FUCI, with whom I
had carried out many pranks, especially against Don
Guano and Don Costa. I'm referring to the engineer
Giancarlo Cevenini, who later became a priest and
who was then working as the cardinal's secretary. In
our first naive request, we also believed that the consecration would take place right away, at the Congress
of Verona, which was slated for the middle of September, and would be attended by a large number of
bishops. I was received by Cardinal Lercaro to whom
I left a publication regarding the desire of Our Lady of
Fatima, as revealed by Lucia, the visionary who was
still living, to the Holy Father, Pope Pius XII.

The cardinal's response was promising. Father Amorth recalls his reply:

> Most Reverend and Dearest Don Amorth,
>   I received your [letter] in a timely manner. I appreciated it very much because it offered me a valuable opportunity to honor Our Lady. I was in Verona for the diocesan Eucharistic Congress on Monday, the fifteenth of the current month. I was there just that day, and as only Archbishop Urbani and the bishop of Comacchio were present, it did not seem to be the appropriate opportunity. Upon reflection, I thought that the matter would enter its rightful place immediately and with certain and complete results if the Italian Episcopal Conference (CEI), which represents the entire Episcopate of the nation, were to take it onto itself. It also seems to me to be the only body that can authoritatively express the thought and will of the Italian Episcopate. Today, 20 September, I have sent a letter, a copy of which I have enclosed, to his Eminence, Cardinal Fossati, president of the conference. Of course, until the CEI communicates its resolution—it will meet soon—the matter should remain highly confidential.

With that, the cardinal of Bologna had fully taken on the initiative and had chosen the path forward. It was not a modest proposal—in effect, improvised and with the agreement of one or two bishops—but an official decision that would involve the entire episcopate. While today such a pathway may appear self-evident, the Italian Episcopal Conference (CEI) in 1958 was a gathering, created somewhat spontaneously, of the presiding bishops of the regions (about twenty). Added to them were the national assistant of Catholic Action, the military ordinariate, and the secretary. The goal was to have the (by then) elderly pontiff, Pope Pius XII, listen to them as a group since he no longer received bishops for ordinary visits. The CEI was, therefore, a recently conceived association. The common sentiment at the time was: "In Italy, we have the pope and there is no need for an [Italian] Episcopal Conference." The CEI had very limited tasks, and it had never taken any initiatives. Notably, their first initiative would be at the behest of Father Amorth, the consecration of Italy to the Immaculate Heart of Mary.

The young Pauline priest would be the cause of action and instrument of Our Lady form early in his priesthood. As he recalls the response of Cardinal Lercaro:

Most Reverend Don Amorth,

I am following up on my previous letter to confidentially communicate the not entirely positive response from His Eminence, Cardinal Fossati. He writes, "I have no difficulty in presenting [the proposal of the consecration] in the short meeting that the Most Eminent cardinals of the CEI will hold on the morning of 21 October before the plenary session. However, I fear that since the topic is not already prepared to be on the agenda, it may meet some opposition—not the proposal itself, but the protocol."

This being the case, I would like to ask you to provide me with all the possible documentation related to the request of the Holy Virgin [of Fatima] with appropriate guarantees of authenticity. As I will also be present at the brief meeting, I could, thus, better polish my proposal and have the request inserted in

the agenda. Then, in the plenary session, I would support it with the appropriate documentation. In fact, it
would be desirable that the vote not pass then, coldly,
but instead with full participation and enthusiasm.
Then, in turn, the Fathers present at the conference—
who are the presidents of the regions—would elicit
the interest all the bishops, and the consecration
would not be merely officially, but truly, the expression of the will of the episcopate in response to the
desire of Mary.

Father Amorth wasted no time in his response: "My
immediate task was clear: to prepare the documentation
requested by the cardinal. Due to the difficulty of the proce-
dure, I was reassured by Monsignor Castelli who trusted in
Cardinal Lercaro's judgment. His predictions later proved
correct. Preparing the documentation for Cardinal Lercaro
was an exciting and uncomplicated task for me, as there
was so much available and abundant published material. It
was a welcome project, also because it gave me the opportunity to draw close to many people who, in addition to
their love for the Virgin Mary, encouraged me in every way,
enthusiastic about the initiative." Sensing his dream would
soon become a reality, he laid out for Cardinal Lercaro five
main lessons from the Fatima apparitions:

1. The letter from Sister Lucy of Fatima to Pius XII
(dated December 2, 1940), in which it is stated that
the celestial protection granted to Portugal, which
was consecrated by its bishops to the Immaculate
Heart of Mary, is proof of the graces that will be
granted to other nations if they make the same consecration. This letter, authoritatively authenticated,

was followed by the declarations of the Portuguese ecclesiastical authorities regarding the graces they attributed to the consecration; attached: a speech by Cardinal Ottaviani, one by Cardinal Agagianian, and the appeal of the bishop of Leiria to all the bishops of the world.

I then began a close correspondence with the bishop of Leiria, Monsignor Pereira Venancio, and met with him several times in Rome. He who was of great help to us. Leiria is the diocese on which Fatima depends.

2. The function of the apparitions of Fatima in relation to Russia and worldwide communism. This is an aspect much studied and with abundant documentation, even if it is not well-known by the general public. I remember with gratitude the help that some Jesuit Fathers of the Russicum [College in Rome] gave me, especially Father Schweigl and Father Wetter.

3. The universal acceptance of devotion to the Immaculate Heart of Mary and of the many consecrations to it. The liturgical feast, after the approval of the apparitions of Fatima; historical precedents; the various "*Peregrinatio Mariae*" [Pilgrimages of Mary]; the "consecrations" made by Pius XII and by bishops from all over the world.

4. Theological foundations of consecration. I found a study by Monsignor Pietro Parente, later a cardinal; in 1958, he was archbishop of Perugia; other studies by Father Spiazzi, Father Roschini, Father Da Fonseca.

5. The clear thought and desire of Pope Pius XII. From many documents, it appeared that Pius XII wished that every nation be consecrated by its

episcopate to the Immaculate Heart of Mary. A few weeks earlier, Cardinal Tisserant had solemnly made himself the spokesman for this desire, participating in the Congress of Lourdes as papal legate (*Osservatore Romano*, 15–16 September, 1958). Therefore, the decision of the Italian episcopate would also appear as a tribute to the vow of the recently deceased great pontiff, and would recall him.

While aware of the presence of the Blue Army (a worldwide association of Catholics who promoted the messages of Fatima in opposition to the Red Army of the atheistic Communion of the Soviet Union) in Italy, he found more support than he had perhaps first anticipated:

> I was aware that there was also a branch of the Blue Army in Italy. While inquiring about it, I learned that the person in charge was a dynamic priest from Padua, the founder of the magazine *Presbyterium*, based in Via del Santo in Padua. I went to see him and hence met Monsignor Strazzacappa. I certainly did not know then that our brief evening encounter would be a decisive influence on all his future ministries, with happy and difficult events that crowned the life of that holy priest. I remember the affection with which he welcomed me. When he learned the reason for my visit, he was moved by profound joy. I believe he intuited right away, albeit vaguely, that many of his desires were about to be fulfilled, for which he had worked very much in the past.

Father Amorth was unaware of how deeply his initiative aligned with that of the Blue Army. In a letter dated November 14, 1958 to Monsignor Strazzacappa, he explained that "the immediate objective of the Blue Army is the consecration of each of its members to the Immaculate Heart; all the more desirable therefore that we arrive at the consecration of our entire nation to the Immaculate Heart of Mary." Our Lady was gathering her forces for this most important initiative. As Father Amorth recalls, "Without knowing one another, we were working toward the same goal." He states, "I did not know that the Blue Army, in the National Conference held in Loreto on 13 July of the same year, 1958, had treated this consecration as its main topic. The conference was chaired by Monsignor Caminada, and the main talk was entrusted to Father Franzi. At the end, Monsignor Strazzacappa sent a concluding telegram to the Holy Father, in which he asked for the consecration of Italy to the Immaculate Heart of Mary as a response to the message of Fatima. The Holy Father responded with his own telegram expressing satisfaction and a blessing." His love for the Blessed Mother was now being taken up into the Pauline charism of spreading the Gospel, and the message of Fatima, through modern means:

> Needless to say, we understood each other. In that first meeting, the monsignor also helped me by speaking to me about the "Marian Connection" [Ita: *Collegamento Mariano*]. Actually, he invited me to take part in its annual meeting, scheduled in Rome on 27 October. He said that he would introduce me and that I would meet many people ready to help. I gladly participated in the meeting in Rome also because I had known Monsignor Costantino Caminada for a long time. For a year, he published a commentary on the Gospel in *Famiglia Cristiana*,

in which I also collaborated. It was the annual meeting of the "Marian Connection." One task was that of planning common points, which all the adherents would work on during 1959. The meeting was opened by Father Franzi, who dealt with two points to put in the program: the restoration of the recitation of the Angelus and greater enthusiasm for the practice of the five Saturdays to Our Lady of Fatima. When it was my turn to speak, I briefly said what I was doing and proposed that the "Connection" get involved in preparations for the consecration of Italy, should it be confirmed [by the CEI].

It would be an understatement to say that everyone present was in immediate agreement. It was far from assuming that the "Marian Connection" would soon be transformed into the "National Committee for the Consecration of Italy." I was pleased to see those priests gathered, mostly religious, of different orders and congregations, yet all in solidarity in their love for Our Lady and in the effort to have her honored by following a certain common line. From that moment onward, I had frequent contacts with Father Franzi. On 23 November, he sent me the official participation of the "Marian Connection" in the consecration initiative, specifying that this participation would involve the commitment to collaborate on behalf of the eight companies of the Marian apostolate, the eight diocesan secretariats, and the twenty-one sanctuaries that were part of the "Connection."

Events moved quickly. I felt like I was attending a show. It was as if so many stones in one mosaic, previously prepared by a higher Will, were coming together in the right place and at the right time

to form a pre-established design. I was able to send
Cardinal Lercaro the documents and an initial list
of participating groups. In addition to those already
mentioned, I enclosed the [list of] participating bishops who had responded to the announcement in
Vita Pastorale. Among them Cardinal Mimmi [arch-
bishop of Naples] stood out. In the Naples cathedral, he repeated the same formula of consecration
pronounced by the Holy Father. As papal legate, he
would then be tasked with reading the official formula in Catania.

Cardinal Lercaro had the idea of linking the Consecration of Italy to the National Eucharistic Congress in Catania. He was inspired by our original idea
about the Verona Congress. The cardinal of Bologna
suggested Catania as the best opportunity in the first
letter of request sent to Cardinal Fossati.

He was no stranger to back-and-forth of politics. "I also
considered involving certain political figures," he wrote,
"in particular the honorable Fanfani, then head of the government, whom I had known since I was at university. The
cardinal wrote to me on 4 November, 1958:

Most Reverend and Dear Father,
    I thank you so much for your documentation and
your notes. Come on 2 December. I will be so happy
to see you and speak about it. I think the request of
His Excellency Fanfani could be useful, perhaps with
a letter addressed to me, because addressing it to the
Episcopal Commission could appear as an official
act, for which the consent of the Cabinet would be
required, etc. If His Excellency Castelli asks for its

insertion into the agenda, fine. As I wrote to you, Cardinal Fossati replied to me that it was not possible to insert the topic, since the agenda had already been made and approved. It will be good, I think, to attach [the list of] those bishops participating in response to the proposal made by *Vita Pastorale.*

He notes how there "were still plenty of difficulties and everything could have been dropped," but persisted with the motto: "The Lord helps those who help themselves." A former poltico and Resistance fighter, Father Amorth was non-plussed in the face of opposition.

In addition to Cardinal Lercaro, the promoter, we already had the full agreement of Monsignor Castelli and Monsignor Parente. I also knew that Cardinal Fossati would have a positive influence. I went to Monsignor Mario Castellano, assistant general of Catholic Action, who not only joined, but promised his full assistance. He would become one of the two vice presidents of the organizing committee and would provide us with a room along Via della Conciliazione where we would establish an office for the months in which to work. I remember that he immediately began to host us for various meetings, in which he took part wearing his beautiful white Dominican habit. Given the *Sede Vacante* [empty chair] due to the death of Pius XII, it seemed to us that we had a Holy Father among us. And we told him so!

No less prompt was the participation of my archbishop, Monsignor Amici of Modena. Also, Monsignor Pintonello, the military ordinariate, immediately joined.

I remember many other meetings during those weeks, which were all very encouraging. I often saw Father Roschini, the best-known Mariologist in Italy; Father Da Fonseca, the foremost historian of the Fatima events; Father Lombardi and Father Rotondi of *Mondo Migliore*; Monsignor Fausto Vallainc of the ACI Press Center; Father Mondrone of *Civiltà Cattolica*, also known for his articles on the *Peregrinatio Mariae*; Don Sturzo, who as a good Sicilian had been particularly moved by the tears of Our Lady in Syracuse; Monsignor Umberto Terenzi, always present at the meetings; and many others, including the likeable figure of Monsignor Novarese, who encouraged me with his optimism and wit.

There was a confident anticipation on the part of those who were aware of the initiative. The CEI would meet between 12 and 14 December, and I had an easy time meeting Cardinal Lercaro, who, when he came to Rome, was a guest of the Benedictines at the Basilica of St. Paul.

The thirteenth day of the month is an important date for Fatima. The first apparition of the Cova da Iria took place on May 13, and so did the apparitions on the following months, until the last one on October 13, made famous by the miracle of the sun. December 13 would be important for the decision on the consecration of Italy, and September 13 for the solemn act of consecration.

I remember well the detailed report, which Cardinal Lercaro gave me verbally on the fifteenth: "I don't know why, when I presented the proposal to the CEI, I felt very excited," he said. "He spoke with extraordinary warmth," Monsignor Amici later confided to me. The fact is that the proposal was received with the desired enthusiasm, unanimously. It was the thirteenth. The next day, 14 December, members of the CEI were received in audience by the Holy Father, who gave his approval to the decision.[38]

The victory for Our Lady was decisive. He recalls the private letter he received from Cardinal Lercaro:

I think that His Excellency Monsignor Caminada has already given you the good news, still however confidential: the CEI has unanimously accepted the proposal to consecrate the nation to the Immaculate Heart of Mary (*et ultra*, because some raised two hands), which will take place, on the initiative and

---

[38]   Father Amorth lists those who supported the initiative: Here I should recall the names of the twenty-three members of the CEI who are responsible for the decision: Cardinal Maurilio Fossati, president, archbishop of Turin; Cardinal Giovanni Battista Montini, archbishop of Milan; Cardinal Ernesto Ruffini, archbishop of Palermo; Cardinal Giuseppe Siri, archbishop of Genoa; Cardinal Giacomo Lercaro, archbishop of Bologna; Cardinal Giovanni Urbani, patriarch of Venice; Cardinal Alfonso Castaldo, archbishop of Naples; Monsignor Luigi Traglia, vicar of Rome; Monsignor Giuseppe Amici, archbishop of Modena; Monsignor Demetrio Moscato, archbishop of Salerno; Monsignor Adelchi Albanesi, archbishop of Viterbo; Monsignor Ugo Camozzo, archbishop of Pisa (on behalf of Cardinal Elia Dalla Costa); Monsignor Norberto Perini, archbishop of Fermo; Monsignor Enrico Nicodemo, archbishop of Bari; Monsignor Sebastiano Fraghì, archbishop of Oristano; Monsignor Giovanni Battista Bosio, archbishop of Chieti; Monsignor Giovanni Ferro, archbishop of Reggio Calabria; Monsignor Arrigo Pintonello, military ordinariate; Monsignor Mario Castellano, assistant Eccl. Gen. of the ACI; Monsignor Pietro Parente, archbishop of Perugia; Monsignor Edoardo Facchini, bishop of Alatri; Monsignor Pasquale Venezia, bishop of Ariano Irpino; and Monsignor Alberto Castelli, secretary of the CEI.

opus of the episcopate, at the next National Eucharistic Congress (September 1959) in Catania. The following day, the Holy Father approved the resolution of the CEI. Now we expect to make it public, and His Excellency Monsignor Castelli will officially notify the bishops. In the meantime, in a meeting in Rome with Monsignor Caminada, we considered meeting, deciding, and organizing the appropriate promotional material and preparing aids to make the consecration more spiritually profound and more concrete. We will also eventually organize, in agreement with the Eucharistic Congress Committee, the solemn celebration.

The formal response of the CEI was more subdued since, in the words of Father Amorth, "preparation required a great deal of accuracy." The official letter was "brief but thorough" and could be summarized in three points:

(1) The CEI had unanimously resolved to consecrate Italy to the Immaculate Heart of Mary. This resolution, inspired by the desire of Pope Pius XII, as was recently highlighted by Cardinal Tisserant in Lourdes, had been approved and encouraged by John XXIII;

(2) The consecration, on the initiative and through the work of the episcopate, would take place in Catania, on the occasion of the National Eucharistic Congress next September;

(3) The "Marian Connection" had set up a committee, chaired by Cardinal Lercaro, to be at the service of the bishops and to facilitate the preparation of the Italian people.

He remained active and vigilant throughout the process:

> For my part, having already been briefed on the decision of the CEI, I felt ready to begin. It was too much for me to keep quiet, and I remember the announcement made on the air by Prof. Rendina after my attendance. I informed the people who were aware of the initiative and were looking forward to a response. I also participated in meetings, led by Monsignor Caminada and Monsignor Castellano, with the goal of establishing initial organizational drafts.
>
> Certainly, I was eagerly awaiting the announcement from the *Osservatore Romano*. At that time, CEI meetings were not announced by the Vatican itself. With regard to the meeting of 12–14 December, the *Osservatore* ran an article on the front page only on the eighteenth in order to publish the pope's speech and include a photo of him surrounded by the participants. There was no mention of the consecration of Italy. Evidently, the desire was for the episcopate to learn about the decision from Monsignor Castelli's letter, as Cardinal Lercaro had written to me. For my part, I proposed an announcement to the *Osservatore* that I had written before knowing about the official letter. My little article was published on the front page on 5 February 1959. In rereading it today, I find it very flawed.

After no little effort, as could be imagined with such an undertaking, the formula began to take shape. Just as he had formerly organized forces in Catholic resistance "in the mountains," Father Amorth had brought together the

Italian bishops and the Blue Army in heeding the call of
Our Lady of Fatima:

> Thus, Monsignor Strazzacappa sent a letter dated
> 22 February calling the committee to Rome for the
> twenty-sixth. Meanwhile, he wrote to the bishop of
> Leiria to make sure the proposal was feasible. He
> received a telegram [from the bishop of Leiria] with
> an affirmative response on the twenty-third, in time
> to bring it to the meeting in Rome. I do not know if
> it was before or after speaking with Cardinal Lercaro
> that he also had the enthusiastic support of Monsi-
> gnor Santin, archbishop of Trieste, for the construc-
> tion of the votive temple. This affirmation was also
> made known during the Rome meeting. The council
> that took place on 26 February was the last held by
> the committee. Afterwards, we were all very busy,
> and there was no longer a need to meet. Among
> my paperwork, I have found the letter of invitation
> from Monsignor Strazzacappa, copied here: "Febru-
> ary 22, 1959 - As established at the last meeting, the
> NATIONAL MARIAN COMMITTEE will meet on
> Thursday 26th at 4.30 PM in Via della Conciliazione,
> 1 (2nd floor). Your Most Rev. is warmly requested to
> speak at the meeting of particular importance. Here
> is the agenda: 1) Consecration and Eucharistic Con-
> gress. 2) Passage of Our Lady of Fatima through the
> 100 cities of Italy. 3) Construction of a remembrance
> temple in Trieste, in honor of the Queen of Italy. 4)
> Manifesto: Angelus Domini, etc. 5) Various."
>
> It would be an understatement to say that the two
> central proposals were received with immense enthu-
> siasm. We believed the idea of the *Peregrinatio* was

inspired: by passing through all the provincial capitals, Our Lady herself would preach the great mission to prepare the Italian people! And so it was.

Father Amorth wasted no time in organizing the plan. It would be by helicopter, a *blue* helicopter suitable for a heavenly queen:

> We immediately got to work to discuss the details. I believe it was the pragmatic Monsignor Strazza who had the idea of using a helicopter as a practical means of transporting the Celestial Pilgrim, while planes would be utilized for longer journeys. I remember the reasons well: there was precious little time for such a long journey; the streets would be too jammed with traffic; there was a need to avoid the long queues of cars that would have followed Our Lady on the way down the street—all which would have taken too much time away from the spiritual work that we proposed. As one can see, these were all practical matters. We also considered that there could be a folkloristic aspect that could pose a danger and needed to be avoided. The results proved immensely better than anyone anticipated. The means of transportation chosen, the helicopter, proved to be the only one suitable to guarantee the itinerary in such a limited timeframe and the punctuality necessary to reach the eager crowds. The Marian mission was characterized by prayer, Masses, confession, communion, and night vigils. None of our churches were sufficient to contain the sheer number of people gathered. Therefore, stadiums, squares, and the open countryside were

utilized for the arrival and departure of Our Lady and often also during her stays.

As for the chronicles of the *Peregrinatio*, I refer to the documentation published in the book, which took its title from a phrase of Pius XII: *Il Pellegrinaggio delle Meraviglie* ["The Pilgrimage of Wonders"] (*Presbyterium*, Rome, 1960). The fact that Our Lady arrived from the sky, in a blue aircraft, also created a pleasant, evocative touch. It was a positive aspect that did not take away from, but added to, the spiritual purpose of the great mission.

Next, the agreement was immediately unanimous regarding the temple in Trieste. It seemed to us that this, too, was a necessary initiative which would continue, tangibly, over time the consecration that had taken place. How much sweat it would cost the monsignor! Later, when I accompanied the statue of Our Lady of Fatima, which Monsignor Pereira Venancio had offered for the new temple, from Venice to Trieste, I was pleased to see Monsignor Giovanni Strazzacappa's name engraved on the pedestal. At that time, there was no mention of the title that would be given to the Trieste temple. I knew that Monsignor Strazzacappa would have liked: "to the Queen of Italy," an expression consistent with the language used by the Blue Army. But he was delighted when the Holy Father himself was asked to choose the title. I believe the request was made by Monsignor Santin. He was very satisfied with the name chosen by Pope John XXIII: "To Mary Mother and Queen." He kept saying: "It really is beautiful! Mary is mother and queen—more mother than queen."

The soldier-turned-Pauline then set to work publicizing the event:

Now informed of our enthusiastic adherence to the two proposals and of the way we planned to implement them, Cardinal Lercaro wrote a long article in the *Osservatore* to announce the initiatives we had prepared and set out the reasons for them: the consecration of Italy, the pilgrimage of Our Lady of Fatima, and the temple in Trieste. The article was published on 19 March.

I still remember my proposal at the committee meeting to use the month of May to prepare the people. My proposal was accepted and, in the absence of other collaborators, it was suggested that I write a "Month of May" booklet for the benefit of parish priests. Our Lady also blessed me in this work. I only had one month to spare, swamped as I was by the rest of my workload. The booklet, *Consacrazione a Maria* [Consecration to Mary], came out and was presented by Cardinal Lercaro. Six editions were printed in two months and were all very useful.

I am also grateful to recall an unforgettable friend, Monsignor Domenico Grandi of Modena, who was commissioned that year by the publisher *Edizioni San Paolo* [Pauline Books and Media, in English] to write a month of May [booklet] focused on the message of Fatima. It was very successful. The archbishop, Monsignor Amici, spoke to the crowd when Our Lady departed from Modena, and could say (with a touch of pride) that the two May booklets that were prepared for the consecration had been written by two people from Modena.

He set up camp in the heart of Rome. As he recalls:

Time was running out. Only someone with the dyna-
mism and faith of Monsignor Strazzacappa could
achieve everything, and he always got it all done.
In Rome, thanks to Monsignor Castellano, we had
opened the "Marian National Committee" office on
the first floor of Via della Conciliazione. That was my
usual place of work over the following months. The
telephone rang constantly, and mail arrived every day
with requests for information regarding the events.
Many bishops and episcopal envoys came to visit us
to prepare the program for their cities. I ran the office
under the directives of Monsignor Strazzacappa,
who took care of everything else. He also dealt with
expenses and remuneration for the necessary aux-
iliary personnel. His "Handmaidens" did excellent
work with the *Peregrinatio*.

I recall when the monsignor came to the office,
just after it opened, carrying addressed envelopes,
paper with letterhead, and other material needed for
the day's work. One morning, his eyes radiant with
joy, he submitted to me the detailed program of the
helicopter trips and the longer flights by plane. The
first would be on 25 April in Naples, followed by a
series of quick flights to the ninety-two provincial
capitals. There would be no possibility of stopping,
and there were many untimely periods. Every day
was vital, and it didn't matter whether it happened
to be a weekday or a Sunday, or May or [the vacation
month of] August. He had put together the itinerary
quickly and unevenly, though it turned out to be fully
appropriate.

He later communicated to me his admiration regarding the complete willingness demonstrated by the entire episcopate. It is true that the CEI had given its resolution and there was the approval of the Holy Father, and it is true that the esteemed figure of Cardinal Lercaro had been appointed to the presidency of the committee. But it is also true that, regarding the execution, it was the two of us, largely unknown and inexperienced, who assigned each city the day and duration of the visit of the Celestial Pilgrim. And yet all the bishops accepted [our decisions] without discussion or protest, but only with gratitude.

Our episcopal and personal contacts with Monsignor Pereira Venancio, bishop of Leiria, Portugal, became frequent. He participated enthusiastically by offering the statue of Fatima for the pilgrimage. He also gave us continual reassurance with his experience: "Our Lady does everything herself"; "There should be an abundance of confessors: there can never be too many"; "Do not worry about preaching." This was all valuable advice.

Only an organizer with zeal and persistence could have put this together. He recalls how the leader of the Blue Army suffered throughout the effort:

It is not surprising that there was no shortage of difficulties in organizing the *Peregrinatio* so quickly. But every diocese was able to overcome the obstacles very well. Where it was most difficult was in Rome. The vicariate was completely immersed in preparations for the Roman Synod desired by the Holy Father. On top of that, they had to continue with their daily tasks, so that thinking about anything else caused serious difficulty. I referred to Monsignor Strazzacappa and I don't know who exactly gave him the job. I just know that he was in charge of providing for everything: "Let him do everything." And he threw himself into it with all his generosity and organizational talents, despite his fatigue and other commitments. He was cheerful. He felt that he was working for Our Lady in the name of the pope since he was preparing everything for the Roman diocese. And so the passage of Our Lady of Fatima through Rome was a great success. Monsignor wrote in his personal notes: "All expectations were surpassed. If the beginning was triumphal, the conclusion in Rome was overwhelming."

Unfortunately, Monsignor Strazzacappa's efforts were misinterpreted, and a great displeasure was inflicted on him. The Lord was preparing him for his eternal reward. After the *Peregrinatio*, the dear monsignor returned to Fatima on 13 October 1959, where he experienced what he referred to as "a mysterious and significant event": just as he set foot in Fatima, he became completely blind. After two days in bed, he flew back to Italy. He resumed his intense and heavy workload until his sudden death at the age of fifty-six on Tiber Island.

Over time, Father Amorth gained the support of other Marian organizations.

Father Mason and Father Scotton volunteered to accompany Our Lady. They made themselves available for all those months with a generosity and boundless spirit of sacrifice. Thus, Our Lady was accompanied by two of her children: one from the Company of Jesus, the other from the Company of Mary. In addition to Father Scotton, the Montfortans provided a young seminarian for office work. He proved a very important collaborator.

One task I took on entirely was that of making provisions for the planes and helicopters. I was able to count on my long friendship with Giulio Andreotti, then minister of defense. To execute it, I was informed of a particular convention that existed between the Republic of Italy and the Sovereign Order of Malta. Here, too, there was an immediate understanding. The Order of Malta took on the initiative directly. I met many times with Prince Rampolla, sometimes alone, other times accompanied by Count Pietromarchi.

Regarding the issue of the airplanes, I was out of the loop on many aspects. I was ignorant of the internal meetings of the Order of Malta, as well as their official relations with the Italian government. I only know that everything turned out well. Of course, no matter how much we tried to forge ahead, negotiations took time, and I was afraid events would not stay on schedule. It was already well into April, and we were still not sure whether we would have the necessary flight arrangements.

Once again, the resolute faith of Monsignor Strazzacappa encouraged me: "You will see: on 25 April, we will have two helicopters, and we will argue over which one to leave parked." In fact, precisely that took place. On 25 April in Naples, for the transportation by helicopter from Capodichino Airport to Piazza

Plebiscito, we had two helicopters at our disposal: that of the fire department and that of the army. Our problem was finding a way not to disappoint one of the two parties.

For the opening of the pilgrimage, I thought it appropriate to invite the head of government, Honorable Segni, who succeeded Honorable Fanfani. Cardinal Lercaro wrote to me on 22 April: "Dearest and most Rev. Fr. Amorth, Today I sent a formal invitation to His Excellency Segni, so that the Government will be represented at the event next Saturday in Naples. As for the invitation to the President of the Republic, I am perplexed, since this is more delicate and involves much more complex entities and matters. It is not a question of welcoming just anyone's enthusiasm without due ponderance. In fact, I cannot proceed with the invitation of the President without the formal and precise consent of the Secretariat of State of His Holiness. If this is given to me, to shorten the time, the Committee can also make the invitation from Rome in my name; otherwise I am sorry, for I shall have to abstain."

Regarding Honorable Segni, I take delight in recalling a particular event, which I personally witnessed with several others. The statue of Our Lady arrived in Rome from Catania. I went to the military airport of Centocelle to pay my respects to her. Before the plane arrived with Our Lady of Fatima, the presidential plane carrying the honorable Segni had landed from abroad. As the president knew that the plane carrying the statue of Our Lady was about to arrive, he remained to wait for her. When he saw the white image coming down the airstairs, he ran over to give her a kiss. He had the spontaneity of a child running to meet his mother.

The strong connection between the apparitions of Fatima and communism are well known. Our Lady appeared in 1917, the same year as the Russian Revolution. While no one could imagine how communism would spread throughout the world, the Fatima messages foretold it, just as they foresaw the immense evil that communism would wreak: atheism taught to the masses, oppression of the person, persecution of the Church, and wars and revolutions throughout the world. But Fatima closed with a message of hope: "In the end, my Immaculate Heart will triumph, Russia will convert, and there will be a long period of peace." The heroic and holy martyr Father Kolbe said prophetically, "You will see the statue of the Immaculata on the highest summit of the Kremlin."

I would have liked to see the powerful pilgrimage not end in Italy, but continue in Austria, Germany, and then beyond the Iron Curtain. As I expressed these wishes to Monsignor Venancio, I was encouraged. He was well disposed to offer his dear statue for new pilgrimages. Therefore, I decided to write to various bishops in Austria and to Cardinal Döpfner, the bishop of Berlin, to inform them of the good that the passage of Our Lady of Fatima was doing in Italy. I was certainly not under the illusion of receiving immediate responses, but I hoped at least to contribute to the preparation of something in the future. I rejoiced immensely when I later learned of the itinerary of the pilgrimage of Our Lady of Fatima across the world, in 1978, especially when I saw that she was going to Vienna, Berlin, and Poland. At last she had crossed the Iron Curtain. When it pleases the Lord, she will arrive in Moscow, and this will be her most beautiful triumph.

Cardinal Lercaro was aware of my ideas and my correspondence. He wrote to me on 21 July: "Dearest Don Amorth, I was in Fatima. I saw the bishop of Leiria, but he did not tell me about the journey of Our Lady to Austria and Berlin. Cardinal Cerejera [the patriarch of Lisbon] instead confirmed to me the authenticity of the promise of the Blessed Woman for the Nations which, following Portugal's example, will consecrate themselves to her Immaculate Heart. Those words are contained in a letter from Lucia (I believe from 1949 or 1950) to the Holy Father, Pius XII, that was passed to the patriarch. The patriarch personally made a copy. Fr. Gonzaga Da Fonseca should be authorized (either by Lucia or by the Holy Father) to publish that promise. The patriarch, moreover, I believe is in favor of granting it, and also the bishop of Leiria, whose appreciation for the Marian Itinerary in Italy is also evident from the invitation made to me to celebrate the Pontifical [Mass] at the Cova da Iria on 13 May next, which is the most solemn day for Fatima and the year in which the secret will be opened. I thank the Lord who inspired you with the idea and you who translated it into action: the ruin of the world is upon us; it is necessary that Our Lady hurry there soon where this ruin is being prepared!"

Two days later, in response to a letter of mine, he wrote to me: "I heard joyfully the news from Austria and Berlin, and I await the letter from Cardinal Döpfner; to add my encouragement to yours."

Saint Padre Pio also came to the event.

I do not know the timing of God. I have the impression that even after all we have seen, the message of Fatima has been poorly received and the Western world is flirting with communism. I trust in the protection of Our Lady over Italy, which is consecrated to her, but consecrations must be lived. They do not act mechanically.

I had been going to Padre Pio for many years. I was his spiritual son, and I wanted the sacred image to make a detour to San Giovanni Rotondo. But the fact that the calendar was packed and already set and communicated to the bishops seemed to make this desire impossible. Instead, the path opened up completely naturally. The stigmatized father would later say [speaking of himself in the third person]: "Our Lady came here because she wanted to heal Padre Pio."

I looked at the calendar at early August when visits near Foggia were scheduled. I noticed that two days had been assigned to Benevento, while other cities had just one day. I felt it was enough for the native province of Padre Pio to have just one day in order to add a visit to San Giovanni Rotondo. I wrote to the bishop and received an affirmative response.

With great pleasure, I communicated my proposal to Father Mariano, my good Capuchin friend, and to the archbishop of Manfredonia, Monsignor Cesarano. The latter was initially against it. In an itinerary so official, limited to the provincial capitals, it seemed to him that an exception should not be made for San Giovanni Rotondo, in that many far more important Italian cities had been excluded. Once again, I turned to the mediation of Cardinal Lercaro, who took care of everything. In a subsequent letter, the archbishop of Manfredonia wrote to me granting his full approval.

Our Lady was using Father Amorth to unite her children in Italy. As was reported by the Capuchins of Pietrelcina in a letter to Father Amorth: "Padre Pio is very happy with the success of your work. I asked him for a word for you, and the Father [Padre Pio] said to me these exact words: 'Tell him that I always remember him with love to the Lord, and I pray to the Heavenly Mother to grant him a great reward in this life and in the next.'"

Biographer of Saint Pio of Pietrelcina, Fr. Fernando da Riese, dedicated a chapter to the event with Our Lady of Fatima. It recounts a miraculous healing through her intercession: "Pio had been ill for months. From 5 May he could neither celebrate Mass nor hear confessions, precisely when there were the largest crowds. As the helicopter departed after the visit, Padre Pio addressed Our Lady with a trusting lament: 'Madonna, Mamma mia, you came to Italy and I got sick. And now you are going away and you leave me still sick.' In that instant, he felt a type of shiver. He said to his confreres: 'I am healed.' He felt as healthy and strong as he ever had."

"The visit to Padre Pio," recalls Father Amorth, "was not the only variation from the official program. There were others. I remember one in Rome, the stop at the hospital of San Camillo, prepared very well by Monsignor Angelini (Monsignor Angelini was correct to remind me of the Virgin's predilection for her sick children). Then there was the very brief stop at the central house of the Pauline

Family, where Don Alberione welcomed the Virgin with his congregations."

THE FORMULA OF CONSECRATION

The formula for consecration went through several revisions, including language for Italians who had immigrated to the United States after the war. The letters below show some of the thought that went into the final formula:

> This, too, was a concern of Cardinal Lercaro. In a letter dated 23 July, he spoke to me about it: "As for the formula of consecration, I wrote something to Monsignor Strazzacappa regarding the tone that it should have, in my opinion. I think we could do it ourselves (like the episcopate's formula). And if the Holy Father gives us one of his own, all the better!"
>
> On 9 August, he wrote to me: "On the sixteenth of this month. I am leaving for the United States and will return not before 2 September. Therefore, I am entrusting to you the task of keeping up to date regarding this matter after my departure. I sent Monsignor Strazzacappa, at the committee address (on Via Conciliazione, 1), a formula of consecration that reflects what I think [it should be]. I have also written to him that I would like it to be examined and, in particular, submitted to His Eminence Cardinal Mimmi who, as papal legate in Catania, will be tasked with eventually reading it. I am so pleased with the good news that continue to arrive from the cities where Our Lady passes. All this is a confirmation that this

was willed by the Lord and a guarantee of the graces that will follow the consecration."

And on 2 August: "Most Reverend and Dearest Don Amorth, I am writing to you about something new, which also seems to me providential. (To summarize: it concerns Italians who have emigrated abroad). It seems wonderful. It would seem to me that the committee, with the consent of the Superior Council of Emigration (Cardinal Mimmi, who is our legate), addressed a letter to all the chaplains of emigrants abroad, to communicate the event of the consecration and spiritually associate it with our emigrated brothers and sisters. Furthermore, I think we could insert into the formula of consecration (it is already long, but it will happen only once!) a reference to emigrants, for example, where it is said: 'to comfort the sufferings, nourish the hopes of the brethren who have been forced by want to cross the borders of their homeland.' As I wrote to you, I am leaving; I leave it to you. I have instructed the Honorable Salizzoni, deputy secretary of the Party, to consult Segni and Gronchi for their role in Catania. I await your reply, and I will send you the letters or the letter, written by hand, so that you can have it/them signed by His Excellency Monsignor Bentivoglio and forwarded."

Cardinal Mimmi was receptive to the suggestion, and he included the reference to emigrants in the final formula of consecration. The consecration was to be carried out most solemnly in Catania, on 13 September, 1959, on the final day of the National Eucharistic Congress.

Pope John XXIII sent a radio message for the closing: "This sentiment of humility and willing service of God and His Church has led you to today's profession of faith and love, which from now on will be more generous than in the past, after the act of consecration of Italy made by you to the Immaculate Heart of Mary. By virtue of this homage to the Blessed Virgin, we trust that all Italians will venerate with renewed fervor in her the Mother of the Mystical Body of which the Eucharist is the symbol and vital center. Let them imitate in her the most perfect model of union with Jesus our Head. May they unite to her in the offering of the divine Victim. And may they beseech through her maternal intercession, for the Church, the gifts of unity, peace, and above all a faithful flourishing and flowering of priestly vocations. In this way, consecration will become a reason for ever more serious commitment in the practice of Christian virtues, an utmost valid defense against the evils that threaten them, and a source of prosperity, even temporal, according to the promises of Christ."

Six days later, on 19 September, the first stone of the Trieste temple was laid with the title *Mary Mother and Queen*, which, as the pontiff himself said, "will remind everyone of the gentle bond of consecration."

THE ACT OF CONSECRATION

Virgin Mary, Mother of God and our Mother, who in Fatima exhorted us to pray, to make reparation for sins, and to consecrate ourselves to your Immaculate Heart, we welcome your invitation with a filial and grateful soul. In this hour full of distress for the entire world, we raise our trusting and fervent prayer to you.

We pray, O Mary, that you obtain for us from Jesus the grace of our salvation and of all humanity so that the world be freed from all hatred, injustice, and violence, so that mankind feels a fraternal bond and lives in harmony and peace.

Looking at our conscience and our works, we recognize ourselves to be sinners and through you we humbly ask the Lord for forgiveness. We have sinned by turning away from God's will and forgetting the promises of baptism. We have not lived the Gospel, and we have not testified to our faith. Obtain for us pardon, O Refuge of sinners.

And now we consecrate ourselves to your Immaculate Heart (or: we consecrate to the Immaculate Heart our family, parish, diocese . . .). May our consecration be an act of total availability to God and His plan of salvation on us, to live by your example and with your maternal guidance. We are aware that this consecration commits us to live according to the demands of baptism, that it unites us to Christ as members of the Church, a community of love, of prayer, of the proclamation of the Gospel in the world.

Accept, O Mother of the Church, this consecration of ours and help us to be faithful to it. With you, humble handmaid of the Father, we will say our yes to the divine will every day of our lives. Through you, Mother and disciple of Christ, we shall always walk in the way of the Gospel. Guided by you, bride and temple of the Holy Spirit, we will spread joy, fraternity, and love in the world.

O Mary, turn your merciful eyes to humanity consecrated to your Immaculate Heart. Implore for the Church, for families, and for peoples the gift of unity and peace. You who already live gloriously in the light of God, offer today's tormented mankind the victory of hope over anguish, of communion over solitude, of peace over violence.

Accompany us in the journey of faith in this life and after this, our exile, show us the blessed fruit of your womb, Jesus. O clement, O loving, O sweet Virgin Mary![39]

---

[39]   Amorth, *Maria. Un sì a Dio*, 203–246.

6

"YOU TAKE CARE OF IT!"

The new pope, John XXIII, announced the year 1959 to be a year of grace. Just three months after his election to the throne of Peter, on Sunday January 25, the Holy Father celebrated the liturgical solemnity of the Conversion of Saint Paul in the Benedictine abbey of Saint Paul's Outside the Walls. At the end of the Mass, in a sort of "unannounced consistory," the pope closed himself off in a room with the cardinals present. Pope John wished to disclose the news of a decision he had made with his closest advisors. He spoke of the Church and her difficulties of the day: weakened spirits, divisions, resistances, being shut off—all in a rapidly changing world that involved matters of the faith. With that, the elderly pope from Bergamo announced to the seventeen cardinals present how he intended to respond to the challenges: "Venerable brothers and beloved sons of ours. We pronounce before you, admittedly trembling a bit with trepidation, but together with humble steadfastness of purpose, the name and proposal of a twofold celebration: that of a Diocesan Synod for the City and of an Ecumenical Council for the universal Church."

A council! The last one was interrupted ninety years earlier, under Pope Pius IX, when the Piedmontese troops of Victor Emanuel II reached the gates of Rome. Pope Pius XI also had the idea, but nothing came to fruition. Even Pope Pius XII considered one but was also unable to realize it. And then the elderly Pope John XXIII, considered by many to be a transitional pope lacking in any significance, announced a council by surprise. Without consulting anyone other than his secretary of state, Cardinal Tardini, he caught everyone off guard. He really wanted a council, and soon, because he knew he didn't have much time. As such, it would begin immediately. The council, in fact, began on Wednesday October 11, 1962. Pope John XXIII would not see it through, however, as he would leave the world before its conclusion. But the door was opened, resulting in much change in the life of the Church and the world.

After the Marian pilgrimage, Father Gabriele Amorth began a period of intense activity within his congregation. Father Alberione instructed him to organize various institutes to add to the Society of St. Paul. He told Father Amorth that there would be "one for priests: the Institute of Jesus Priest; one for men: the Institute of St. Gabriel the Archangel; and one for women: the Institute of Our Lady of the Annunciation. He entrusted them to me and told me: 'You take care of it!'"[40] This command was typical of Father Alberione, who would identify a goal, entrust it to one of his members, and then send him or her to accomplish it, empty-handed, like the disciples of Jesus. The founder trusted in God and His providence—something Father Amorth would

---

[40]   Fezzi, *La Mia Battaglia Contro Satana*, 21.

carry with him for the remainder of his priestly ministry. Father Amorth explained Father Alberione's vision and the meaning of these additional institutes: "For the Institute of Jesus Priest, he clearly saw the need to remove diocesan priests from isolation and give them the possibility of living full religious vows, while remaining in their [clerical] state. For the two lay Institutes—the Institute of St. Gabriel the Archangel and the Institute of Our Lady of the Annunciation—he saw above all two purposes: to bring total consecration to God into all life professions, in every environment; and a response to atheism of the day."[41]

Father Amorth remained at Father Alberione's side until the latter's death in 1971. His spiritual father had entrusted into his hands the three new institutes, which he subsequently accompanied for a long time. Father Amorth would tell Elisabetta Fezzi, "The male and the female ones were just conceived and were a small group of people. The one for priests, on the other hand, had yet to begin. So I had to go and look for priests who would come take a course of spiritual exercises and talk to them about this institute, hoping they would enter. And so we began."[42]

Once again there is evidence of Father Amorth as a pioneer, a sower with a field to bear fruit. He threw himself into the new institutes with enthusiasm, achieving good results: "Then, a little at a time [the priests] grew in number. This was the most demanding institute. I stepped down and entrusted it to Father Lamera. He had great communion with the priests, and was, in fact, a great grace for them. Then I also stepped down from the St. Gabriel the Archangel Institute because I couldn't do it anymore. By

---

[41]   Gaeta, *L'eredità segreta di don Amorth*, 13.
[42]   Fezzi, *La Mia Battaglia Contro Satana*, 21.

then, there were almost three hundred *Annunziatine* [a colloquial term for women of the Institute of Our Lady of the Annunciation] and I was constantly going around preaching spiritual exercises and giving retreats."[43]

After seventeen years tirelessly accompanying the institutes, his congregation called him to a new internal assignment. After the death of the founder, the Paulines were led by his successor, Fr. Luigi Zanoni, until 1975. Later, Fr. Raffaele Tonni took over. In 1977, he asked Father Amorth to take on the provisional role of provincial delegate:

> He did not want to appoint a provincial superior for Italy, but a delegate because he had ideas he wanted to develop, and he needed an executor. So I left the *Annunziatine* and became provincial delegate. That was my most difficult year, the most painful, because I never had those gifts and was not suited to it. I was not prepared for that task. So from my point of view, it was a very bad year. The positive aspect is that it separated me from the Our Lady of the Annunciation Institute. If not, I would still be there! Instead, I detached myself and became available for something else.[44]

He then moved on to look after the Pauline cooperators—lay people who shared the ideals of Father Alberione and his congregation. These men and women worked closely with the Society of St. Paul in diverse ways, "with the Pauline spirit, as indicated by the Founder, with prayer, with works and with offerings." Father Amorth would

---

43   Fezzi, 21.
44   Fezzi, 21–22.

accompany them for a year before given a new task. He explained, "Then Don Zilli, the director of *Famiglia Cristiana*, died. Following his death, the magazine needed help. Then the superior general, Don Renato Perino, called me and said, 'I need to send Don Andreatta (who was then editor-in-chief of [the magazine] *Madre di Dio* [Mother of God]) to Milan to *Famiglia Cristiana* and, if you accept, I shall entrust you with *Madre di Dio*.'"[45]

Father Giuseppe Zilli, from Fano Adriano in the region of Abruzzo, born in 1921, was behind one of the most extraordinary editorial ventures in the history of Italy. He took over as director of *Famiglia Cristiana* in 1954 when it was little more than a religious paper distributed in parishes, and he transformed it into a bastion of two million copies. He made it a highly influential magazine in the world of modern media. He brought in lay journalists, modernized the printing apparatus in Alba, updated the graphics, and moved the main editorial office to Milan from Alba (which was too secluded). He contributed personally to it in a column of readers' letters called *Colloquies with the Father* (*Colloqui col Padre*). It was rich in experiences, ideas, advice, and concrete help.

Father Zilli also created *Jesus*, a monthly magazine dedicated to news and religious culture, in which intellectuals from the Catholic world and other religions collaborated. The cover of the first issue remains famous. It depicted Jesus in a suit and tie, signifying the need to update the eternal message of the Gospel. He also founded the *Gruppo Periodici Paolini*, which today is called *Periodici San Paolo*, and became its general director. Generations of journalists grew up under his leadership. He chose as his

---

45   Fezzi, 22.

vicar his confrere and friend, Fr. Leonardo Zega, from the province of Macerata in the Marche region to succeed him as director. Father Zilli also founded a radio and a television channel. He remains the quintessential Pauline priest, committed to spreading the Gospel with every modern means of communication.

Each week, he would travel from Milan to Alba and back, in every season, to close out his column in the print shop. He was a dangerous driver, to the point that people would say that the Paulines had a fourth vow: "speed." Just before Christmas, in 1978, on his return to Milan, he had a very serious accident on the motorway. He survived, but his long ordeal through the hospitals began. The numerous treatments and operations weakened his robust physique. After he recovered, he returned to work, though his voice was tired. In 1980, he participated in the general chapter of the Society of St. Paul in Ariccia near Rome. He was spoken of as a possible candidate for the role of superior general. But he died suddenly, at just fifty-eight years old, on March 31, Holy Monday, probably from a heart attack caused by consequences of the accident. His remains were brought to Alba on Good Friday and greeted by thousands of people in the print shop. He is buried in the Pauline cemetery.

The death of Father Zilli, therefore, led to Father Amorth becoming director of *Madre di Dio*, a Marian magazine run by San Paolo. He recalled:

I had already been editor of this magazine while I was in Alba, so I was not a rookie in the field. I immediately said, "Well, for the Mother of God, one should do this and more!" When I became director, I also dedicated myself to other activities of a Marian nature, such as bringing together the various groups.

We did so many things. The last one, or at least one of the largest, was on 25 March 1984, when Pope John Paul II brought a statue of Our Lady of Fatima to the square, the one that never moves and remains fixed. He brought her for the consecration of the world to the Immaculate Heart of Mary. For the occasion, I gathered all the Marian groups to Saint Peter's Square. There was such a full house in the square that many people were unable to see the pope even from a distance, so crowded was Via della Conciliazione and everything behind Bernini's colonnade. We organizers were in the front row! I could have reached out while the pope was on his knees consecrating the world to the Immaculate Heart of Mary! I could have reached out and touched him! And then he received us in the Chapel of the Pietà, because when he held public gatherings in Saint Peter's Square, he would reenter the door of the basilica, go to the Chapel of the Addolorata which is the first on the right, and then take the elevator up, remove his vestments, and come back down. So he received us there.[46]

Once again, Mary. Father Amorth continued his filial relationship with the Mother of God, now managing a newspaper dedicated entirely to her and promoting consecration. He would do so for eight years, until 1988. He gathered the Marian movements into a special committee, over which he was appointed secretary. The group's president was another man in love with the Virgin Mary, the future president of Italy (1992–99), Oscar Luigi Scalfaro. He, too, had worked on the consecration of the world to Mary in 1984.

---

[46]   Fezzi, 22–23.

Father Amorth's life was under the mantle of the Mother of God, as in the ancient Marian prayer: "*Sub tuum praesidium confugimus, sancta Dei Genetrix*" (We flee under your mantle, Holy Mother of God). Yet, Our Lady had a new mission waiting for her faithful son.

7

AT THE CARDINAL'S HOME

"Ii 1986, my life changed," said Father Amorth. It was a radical, unexpected change, one he had neither imagined nor sought. As with Father Alberione years earlier, his new mission came about again through another providential encounter. A chance encounter with the papal vicar general for [the Diocese of] Rome, Ugo Poletti, would place Father Amorth in a new vineyard. Here is how he recounted the episode to Paolo Rodari:

> I was in the apartment of Cardinal Ugo Poletti, vicar of Rome. Everyone knows that the bishop of Rome is the pope. But from the sixteenth century, the pontiff delegated its pastoral governance to a vicar. It was 11 June, 1986.
>
> Poletti was known for receiving priests without appointments. That day, I, too, following praxis, showed up without an appointment and was immediately received. I didn't have anything in particular to ask my bishop, I just wanted to chat. This is often

what priests need. Poletti was aware of this and never expected that priests should have an important reason to knock on his door.

He asked me about my work within the Society of St. Paul. I was, in fact, a Pauline priest. I was also a lawyer, a passionate Mariologist, a professional journalist, and chief editor of the monthly *Madre di Dio*. I cannot explain why, but at a certain point, the conversation turned to Fr. Candido Amantini. For thirty-six years, he had been the official exorcist of the Diocese of Rome.

"Do you know Father Candido?" Poletti asked me out of the blue.

"Yes," I answered. "I have been to the site where he does exorcisms, out of curiosity—at the Sanctuary of the Holy Stairs, which is located a few steps from here. I have met him. Every now and then I go see him."

As a cardinal, Poletti was quite capable of governance and was decisive. When he made decisions, he immediately put them in writing, with a legible signature and stamp at the bottom of the page. I was surprised when, without explanation, he opened his desk drawer, took out a sheet of paper with diocesan letterhead and began to write. He wrote for about a minute. Just a few lines written in black ink. Then he pulled out a stamp and marked the paper with a single jab at the bottom right. I didn't dare ask anything. Something came to mind, but I immediately dismissed it and waited for him to speak.

"Very well," said the Cardinal, folding and placing the sheet in an envelope, which he left unsealed before handing it to me.

"This envelope is for you. Well done. I know you will do well."

For a few moments, I didn't know what to say. As I received the envelope, I was reminded of what my spiritual father always told me while I was in seminary: "How do you know if you are doing God's will? You can be sure you are on the right path only if you obey your bishop."[47]

That envelope contained Fr. Gabriele Amorth's destiny. "Alberto the Partisan" had a radically new mission. His new assignment in the vineyard of the Lord, something completely different from what he had ever done. He would be an exorcist. As his life by now was revealing, the ways of the Eternal Father are always inscrutable, surprising, shocking.

Being an exorcist is a demanding, consuming, and exhausting trial. The Pauline journalist and priest, in love with the Virgin Mary, now had a new challenge. He knew that this would be formidable and exhilarating, but also tiring and, in many ways, difficult. He was about to look at evil in the face and fight against it with all his might, and for the remainder of his priesthood. Father Gabriele found himself as pioneer once again. He would come to organize another band of spiritual, Catholic Resistance fighters which would shape not simply the future of Italy but the entire Roman Catholic Church herself.

Father Amorth said, "I decided to open the envelope in front of the cardinal. I saw just what I thought it would say. There were just a few rather eloquent words:

Rome, June 11, 1986
I, Cardinal Ugo Poletti, vicar archbishop of the city of Rome, hereby appoint as exorcist of the

47   Amorth, *L'Ultimo Esorcista*, 11–12.

diocese, Fr. Gabriele Amorth, a religious of the Society of St. Paul. He will work alongside Fr. Candido Amantini for as long as is necessary.

In faith,

Card. Ugo Poletti

vicar archbishop of Rome

"But Eminence . . ." Father Amorth protested. Cardinal Ugo Poletti was direct:

Dear Father Gabriele, you do not need to say anything. I have made my decision, and so it must be. The Church is in dire need of exorcists. Rome above all. There are too many people who suffer from possession, and no one has been tasked with freeing them. Father Candido has been asking me for help for some time. But I have always prevaricated, as I did not know whom to send. When you told me you knew him, I knew I could no longer delay. You will do well. Do not be afraid. Father Candido is a special teacher. He will know how to help you.

"I remained speechless," recalled Father Gabriele. Yet he still queried, "I knew the Gospel well. I knew that Christ has given the power to cast out demons to the apostles and their successors, which the bishops, in turn, can delegate to simple priests. I knew that the Church cannot be without exorcists and there are so many people possessed in the world. But, I wondered, would I be able to do it? Why me? Why was I entrusted with such a difficult and dangerous task?"[48]

---

[48]   Amorth, 13–14.

Why me? This is the question of the ages that everyone asks themselves in life. The answer is in the wind, the Spirit of God, in His extraordinary designs. Who knows why Cardinal Poletti had that inspiration. The Pauline priest who stood before him had never had any experiences with the devil, nor did he know anything about exorcisms. The obedient son of the Church and faithful servant of Our Lady, however, moved quickly from *why me* to *why not me*? It was his turn. And since he knew he had to always obey his bishop, Father Amorth left his bishop's home with his letter in hand and countless questions in his heart and mind. He would not refuse. Instead, he reflected on what he knew to be true:

> The struggle between good and evil, between Satan and Christ, goes back to the beginning. Two armies have always fought for supremacy over the world: the army of Satan and the army of Christ. No one knows why Satan exists, why one of the most beautiful and noble angels in heaven decided at some point to rebel against God, becoming the prince of darkness. The fact is that he, Satan, exists and wants only one thing: to bring the world to self-destruction and man to eternal damnation. In this seemingly endless struggle, the pope has a key role. It is he, perhaps first and foremost, who must fight so that the gates of hell do not prevail against the Church. Together with him are men of good will who are part of the Church. Among men, a special role is played by exorcists. They are like the tips of diamonds in this army that counters evil with good. They are priests chosen to drive out the extraordinary presence of Satan and his army—the

demons hierarchically subjugated to Satan—from man and, therefore, from the world.

"But," he wondered, "why did I have to be one of these?" Letter of assignment in hand and filled with many questions and some fear, he left the cardinal's office.

As he left the office, he realized that there was only one sensible thing to do—that is, to pray.[49] Father Amorth later told Elisabetta Fezzi that he tried to resist Cardinal Poletti, that he went back to him to "keep him happy." He used various excuses, such as: "But you know me, you know that I am a joker, a good-for-nothing, someone who jokes and pranks."[50] But it was no use. The cardinal had chosen him, even with his character and temperament. Indeed, perhaps he chose him precisely because he was capable of joking and jesting and had a cheerful spirit. What better opponent for the devil with his insidious plots?

As he had learned throughout his entire life, he knew that prayer is the only thing one can do in moments of such great confusion and disruption: pray and ask for help from the only One who can give it. Ask for light to see beyond the shadows of a decision that strike fear in the heart. In that moment of prayer, as he sought refuge on holy ground, he moved from *why not me* to *how*. How can I accomplish this enormous task? How does one fight the devil? How can a man fight against an angel who rebelled against God? Yes, all he could do was pray, fervently and immediately. As he recalls:

> The basilica of Saint John in Lateran is the oldest and most noble in Rome. One of the side chapels always

---

49   Amorth, 14–15.
50   Fezzi, *La Mia Battaglia Contro Satana*, 23.

keeps the Blessed Sacrament, the Body of Christ, exposed. I entered and knelt at one of the wooden benches. And there I made my request to heaven, or rather to Our Lady.

"Mother of God, I accept this assignment, but protect me with your mantle."

It was a simple plea with a few, but heartfelt, words. I wanted to obey my bishop, and I placed all my fears in the hands of Our Lady.

"Who am I to fight the prince of darkness?" I asked. I was no one. But God is everything. The devil is not fought with one's own strength, but with that of heaven.

In that side chapel, as he knelt before the Blessed Sacrament in prayer, Our Lady undoubtedly comforted him with his own words preached at his first sermon. "The mission of a priest," he stated on the day of his ordination, "is beyond human abilities, but [the priest] must not be dismayed by this: to carry out his work, he is granted an overabundance of graces which will never fail him. Therefore, even a petty and unsuitable man, by the mere fact of being a priest, is equipped with a supernatural strength that allows him to accomplish exceptional things."

Now he really had the opportunity to put faith into action. Some time after making that plea in the basilica of Saint John in Lateran, Father Amorth found himself exorcising a possessed person for the first time. He recalls the encounter:

Through his voice, Satan was speaking to me. He spat out insults, blasphemies, accusations, and threats.

Then, at a certain point, he said to me: "Priest, go away. Leave me alone."

"You go away," I responded to him.

"Please, priest, go away. I can do nothing against you."

"Tell me, in the name of Christ, why can you not do anything?"

"Because you are too protected by your Lady. Your Lady with her mantle surrounds you, and I cannot reach you."[51]

Sub tuum praesidium confugimus (Under your mantle we take refuge). This ancient prayer of the Church from AD 254 now became this modern exorcist's battle cry. In a small side chapel of the basilica of Saint John in Lateran, before the Blessed Sacrament—that is, with Jesus physically present, in the presence of Mary His Mother—Fr. Gabriele Amorth accepted a terrible burden: to go to the front lines and fight against Satan himself. The Paulist priest committed to the proclamation of the Gospel would not just proclaim, he would cast out demons, according to the words of Jesus who told the disciples "in my name, you will cast out demons" (Mk 16:17). He would do just that, and he would do it in our century when Satan seems to have won largely by convincing man that he no longer exists.

He stepped down as editor-in-chief from *Madre di Dio* to devote himself exclusively to exorcisms, a task he would perform until the end of his days. He would perform exorcisms, speak, write, and instruct others in the ministry. He always considered himself an instrument in the hands of

---

[51]   Amorth, *L'Ultimo Esorcista*, 15–16.

God, protected and guided by Mary: "I am attached to the Madonna, I am attached to her mantle."

"At that point," he later recounted, "my life changed." How does one begin to be an exorcist? Father Amorth went to Fr. Candido Amantini, who read the letter from Cardinal Poletti. Without any reaction, Father Candido told him, "Good. Let's get started right away. You have to do two things. First. Get an exorcism ritual. It is in Latin. Read the twenty-one rules that precede the Rite. Commit them to memory. Without those rules, you will be defeated. Second. Start [practicing] exorcisms at home, by yourself."[52]

That was his training. Read some rules in Latin and practice exorcisms alone. With that, the apprentice exorcist (again) obeyed. "I studied the twenty-one rules," he said, making note that "I was impressed with the first ones, which are general teachings. They explain that we should never believe that anyone who claims to be possessed actually is. Most people have severe psychological problems. Together, [the rules] teach that the devil is in hiding and that, therefore, it is necessary to possess much prudence, but also to be very smart. The devil must be hunted down."[53]

He would become a hunter who knew the authentic signs of enemy activity. Something else needed to be immediately clear in his mind: "What are the signs of the presence of the devil? Speaking unfamiliar languages fluently or understanding others who speak them; knowing distant or hidden facts; showing strength superior to one's age or natural condition, and other phenomena of this kind."[54]

Thus did Father Amorth follow the instruction of Father Candido and study an exorcist and trained at home,

---

[52]   Amorth, 20.
[53]   Amorth, 20.
[54]   Amorth, 20.

by himself: "I learned the formulas of the ritual well. And when I learned them, I began to intervene on the possessed, first with Father Candido at my side and then alone. I learned the tricks of the trade from Father Candido."[55]

An extraordinary venture of good versus evil thus began. It was the struggle of a jokester and prankster priest against the prince of this world. It would seem an unequal match. But the priest had the Mother of God on his side. "That is when my life changed," he said.[56]

---

[55]   Amorth, 20.
[56]   Fezzi, *La Mia Battaglia Contro Satana*, 23.

8

PETER AND THE SMOKE OF SATAN

he Church now had one more exorcist. At that time, there were very few exorcists, only about twenty in all of Italy. Some, perhaps, believed the fight against Satan was lost from the start. Others, even in the Vatican, believed the notion that Satan did not exist, or no longer existed. And yet, one pope after another stood guard against the Church's infernal enemy. Pope John XXIII certainly did. And how can we forget the words of Paul VI, who spoke of the devil on at least three occasions?

On June 29, 1972, the feast of the Apostles Peter and Paul, Pope Paul VI was speaking of the situation of the post-conciliar Church, of all the anxieties that now followed a season of hope. His words were striking, out of the ordinary, and terrible:

> I have the sensation that from some fissure the smoke of Satan has entered the temple of God. There is doubt, incertitude, problematic, disquiet, dissatisfaction, confrontation. There is no longer trust of the

Church . . . There was the belief that after the council there would be a day of sunshine for the history of the Church. Instead, it is the arrival of a day of clouds, of tempest, of darkness, of research, of uncertainty . . . We believe in something that is preternatural that has come into the world precisely to disturb, to suffocate the fruits of the ecumenical council, and to impede the Church from breaking into the hymn of joy at having renewed in fullness its awareness of itself.

Some in the Catholic world reacted with surprise and unease at the Holy Father's words. Really, the devil? No one talks about him anymore—not in the confessionals, nor from the pulpits. He has even disappeared from the liturgical formulas. Why is the pope referring to him again? The response: because the Gospel speaks about him. Thus some objected, believing that it was better to keep the devil on the sidelines a little bit to give space to other more urgent, fashionable, and engaging issues. Others believed it was wrong to mention the name of the devil in vain. In fact, many in the Catholic world believed that Pope Paul VI was wrong, that he was returning to obsolete, timeless, useless, and unnecessarily divisive issues.

But he repeated himself again five months later. On November 15, at the Wednesday audience in Nervi Hall, he said, "One of the greatest needs of the Church today is to defend itself against that evil we call the devil. He is a terrible reality. [He is] mysterious and fearful . . . Just saying this name, in our time, can seem simplistic, or even superstitious and not real."

There is no getting around it. Those who wish to respect Tradition, the "framework of biblical and ecclesial teaching"—that is, those who want to stay within the confines of the Catholic Church—must take note of and accept this reality: Satan acts in humanity and in the world. The pope continued, "He is the number one enemy, he is the tempter *par excellence.* We know that this dark, contorted being truly exists and still operates with treacherous cunning. He is the hidden enemy who sows errors and misfortunes in human history." Pope Paul VI argued on the reality of personal evil. "Evil," he argued, "is no longer just a deficiency, but an efficiency, a living, spiritual, perverted, and perverting being."

Like Jesus speaking to the disciples at Emmaus, the Holy Father continued explaining the Scriptures by citing them, the Fathers of the Church, and modern authors. He offered several reasons on why this subject was ignored in the post-conciliar Church and world: "The presence of Satan is a very important chapter within Catholic doctrine to restudy, while today he is little [studied] . . . Today one prefers to appear strong and without prejudice, to pose as positivists, except to then believe in so many gratuitous magical or popular superstitions, or worse to open one's soul . . . to the libertine experiences of the senses, to the deleterious [experiences] of drugs, as well as the ideological seductions of fashionable errors, these cracks through which the Evil One can easily penetrate and alter the human mentality."

It seemed as if the pope were recalling the ancient prophecies of his namesake: "For the time will come when people will not tolerate sound doctrine but, following their own desires and [itching ears] will accumulate teachers" [2 Tm 4:3]. This is indeed what happens.

Pope Paul VI would return again to speak of the devil in another general audience on February 3, 1977. "It is not a wonder," he said, "that Scripture bitterly warns us that

the whole world lies under the power of the Evil One."
Father Amorth commented on the evil one the pope called
a "living, spiritual, perverted, and perverting being" as not
contained to the world and culture. He was now actively
militating within the Church: "Paul VI often speaks of the
devil. And he often links him to the Church. Why? Perhaps because he simply wished to admonish the Church,
to ask her to be prudent, to flee the temptations of Satan.
But there is more, in my opinion. Paul VI somehow realizes that Satan is inside the Church, perhaps even inside the
Vatican. He is sounding the alarm."[57]

In 1978, at the death of Pope Paul VI and after the
thirty-three-day pontificate of Pope John Paul I, an unexpected pontiff appeared at the loggia of Saint Peter's Basilica. His name was Karol Wojtyla. He came from Poland,
choosing the name John Paul II. He would be at the helm
of the Barque of Peter for more than twenty-six years and
usher the Church into the third millennium. He, too,
believed in the devil.

Father Amorth explained to Paolo Rodari, "During
his long pontificate, John Paul II fought several times
against Satan. And his battle continues even now that he is
deceased. In fact, John Paul II is still present today during
many exorcisms."

The pope who came from a distant country was a formidable enemy of the prince of this world. Father Amorth
further testified:

> Satan once spoke to me at length about John Paul
> II. I still remember the hoarse voice of the prince
> of darkness. He spoke to me just before he left the

---

57   Amorth, *L'Ultimo Esorcista*, 190.

person he had possessed. It was like a confession he wanted to make to me before I was able to drive him out with the power of Christ. Of course, his words may have been a lie. But they still deserve to be repeated because they tell us something. He said, "Karol Wojtyla, I hate him. We all hate him. Wojtyla destroyed my plans. I wanted to destroy the world, but it was he who made communism fall in Russia and Eastern Europe before I succeeded in my project. Those were years in which entire countries lived in terror. I put them in a permanent state of terror. The Second World War was a masterpiece of mine. But what followed later—communism with millions of deaths and above all the hunger and suffering of entire populations—was icing on the cake that surpassed the cake itself in delectability. The Pole helped bring the light back. And he took many young people out of my hands. They were mine. I initiated them into evil. They lived for me, some knowingly, some unknowingly. He took them from me. I hate him for it. And I will hate him forever."[58]

There are anecdotes of exorcisms done by the pope himself, though his name is enough to trigger the reaction of Satan. Father Amorth notes the reaction of the devil when Pope John Paul II and Padre Pio are invoked during an exorcism. "When John Paul II is named during an exorcism," observes Father Amorth, "the possessed literally foams with anger . . . When Padre Pio of Pietrelcina is named, the devil goes mad and becomes furious and agitated. But when John Paul II is named, Satan becomes

---

[58]   Amorth, 187–88.

even more brutal and uncontrollable. Satan hates John Paul II and often says, 'I hate him with greater intensity than Padre Pio.'"[59]

Therefore, concludes Father Amorth, "John Paul II was fundamental for us exorcists. He gave us back our place in the Church after oblivion had fallen upon us for centuries. He always said to the Church: 'Whoever in the Church does not believe in the devil does not believe either in the Gospel.' Wojtyla believed in the existence of Satan. And he completely trusted in Christ. Others in the Vatican have not done so, and perhaps continue in that vein."[60]

Pope Benedict XVI is also considered very powerful by the devil. As Monsignor Andrea Gemma stated in the book *Confidenze di un esorcista* (*Revelations of an Exorcist*), during an exorcism, [the devil] said, "The old man (referring to John Paul II) did enormous damage to us, but the one there now is worse." The one there now was, in fact, Joseph Ratzinger, who succeeded Pope John Paul II in 2005 with the name Benedict XVI. A few days before ascending to the throne of Peter, in the meditations for the Via Crucis at the Colosseum, he pointed his finger at the "filth" inside the Church. He certainly knew what he was talking about. For years, he held the uncomfortable and pivotal role of Prefect of the Doctrine of the Faith, the congregation formerly known as the Holy Office, where Catholic doctrine is upheld. Here, all the miseries of the life of the Church were discharged—and still are.

As pope, he did not perform exorcisms, but, as Father Amorth would say, Pope Benedict XVI "was feared by Satan" due to his life and his faith, and his faithful service to the

---

[59]   Amorth, 188.
[60]   Amorth, 188–89.

Church. Father Amorth recalled how Joseph Ratzinger was an unbearable enemy of the devil, notably in the reverence of how he said Holy Mass: "The way in which Benedict XVI performs the liturgy, his respect for the rules, and his rigor and posture are very effective against Satan. The liturgy celebrated by the pontiff is powerful. Satan is wounded every time the pope celebrates the Eucharist."[61] After the resignation from the pontificate in February 2013, Father Amorth recognized that "Pope Benedict XVI has done many things for exorcists, starting with the drafting of the *Catechism of the Catholic Church*, and for allowing us exorcists to be able to administer the sacramental of exorcism not only to people who suffer diabolical possession, but also to those who suffer from diabolical disturbances, such as diabolical vexation and infestation."[62]

Satan did not want Ratzinger to be pope, and he had reason. But it was certainly not better with his successor, Jorge Mario Bergoglio. Pope Francis was elected on March 13, 2013, chosen "from the ends of the earth." He has often expressed himself clearly about the devil and his real presence in the world and in the Church itself. In his apostolic exhortation *Gaudete et Exsultate*, he wrote that the devil is not "a myth, a representation, a symbol, a figure of speech or an idea." No, Pope Francis stated that he is a present and powerful being: "We will not admit the existence of the devil if we insist on regarding life by empirical standards alone, without a supernatural understanding. It is precisely the conviction that this malign power is present in our midst that enables us to understand how evil can at times have so much destructive force." We must not be

---

[61]   Amorth, 183–84.
[62]   Public comment of Fr. Gabriele Amorth regarding the renunciation of the papacy of Benedict XVI, February 2013.

deceived and "let down our guard, to grow careless and end up more vulnerable." And again: "[Satan] does not need to possess us. He poisons us with the venom of hatred, desolation, envy and vice. When we let down our guard, he takes advantage of it to destroy our lives, our families and our communities."

In a homily of the Pentecost Mass, on May 23, 2021, Pope Francis again warned against the presence of the devil:

> Dear sisters, dear brothers, if you feel the darkness of solitude, if you feel that an obstacle within you blocks the way to hope, if your heart has a festering wound, if you can see no way out, then open your heart to the Holy Spirit. St. Bonaventure tells us that, "where the trials are greater, he brings greater comfort, not like the world, which comforts and flatters us when things go well, but derides and condemns us when they do not" (Homily in the Octave of the Ascension). That is what the world does, that is especially what the hostile spirit, the devil, does. First, he flatters us and makes us feel invincible (for the blandishments of the devil feed our vanity); then he flings us down and makes us feel that we are failures. He toys with us. He does everything to cast us down, whereas the Spirit of the risen Lord wants to raise us up.

There is no ambiguity on behalf of the successors of Saint Peter. The devil remains the number one enemy for all children of God. He is behind the denials and betrayals of faith, the great and small sins that wound the whole of humanity, weakening man and rendering him defenseless, fragile, and impotent. He is behind the sufferings inflicted by man against man, behind the frightening tragedies of war, violence, and arbitrariness carried out every day against the smallest, humblest, poorest, simplest creatures. He is always there in the divisions, in wickedness, in selfishness that divide men among themselves, in the blood poured out between fathers and children, brothers, and spouses. He is a cancer that destroys human coexistence.

9

"I AM LUCIFER"

At the age of sixty, and with this backdrop, the life of Fr. Gabriele Amorth radically changed, and his new battle began. From then on, his mission was at the front lines in a struggle against evil, face-to-face with mankind's number one enemy himself. He did not ask for such an assignment, nor had he planned for it. Nonetheless, these are the ways of God. He said, "This is how I became known as an exorcist, while, to tell the truth, I was a Mariologist." He added with humor that he was a "Mariologist (*mariologo*) and not a thief (*mariuolo*), as someone once referred to me! My subject is Mariology, I am attached to the Madonna, I am attached to her mantle."[63] And so, attached to Mary's mantle, Father Gabriele began an unexpected and unforeseen career, which would last thirty years, until his last day on earth.

As noted above, he began by studying and learning the twenty-one rules of exorcism, written in Latin and "not

---

63 Fezzi, *La Mia Battaglia Contro Satana*, 24.

accessible to everyone, only to exorcists."[64] The rules serve to understand the foundational elements of the praxis of exorcism which, at heart, is true warfare. For example, some words are most effective at embarrassing the enemy. These should be used more often in order to annoy and weaken him. After all, the devil takes countermeasures in an attempt to mislead the exorcist. Like in any battle, there is back and forth. As Father Amorth says, "They usually respond with lies. They manifest themselves in a difficult way for the exorcist. After he tires, they try to get [the exorcist] to give up. Or the victim pretends to be ill and not possessed by the devil."[65]

Diversion is a common tactic. The evil one sometimes hides to lead the exorcist to think he has defeated him. In sum, he tries to divert attention away from himself. Since this in an action of the Church, an exorcism must, therefore, be performed in a church or annexed room, strictly out of public view. In case of illness of the possessed, it can be on occasion done in one's home. Superstition, anything contrary to true religion, must be avoided at all costs. Thus, explains Father Amorth, "Some possessed people say they have received a curse, and they also say by whom it was cast and in what way, according to them, it can be overcome. But it is important to be careful that in doing so they do not turn to magic, or sorcerers, or others, rather than resorting to the ministers of the Church. One must not resort to any form of superstition or other illicit means."[66]

Father Amorth is quick to remind Catholics that they should never forget that the devil is defeated by God, not by man. The exorcist is merely the instrument, while the one

---

[64]   Amorth, *L'Ultimo Esorcista*, 20.
[65]   Amorth, 21.
[66]   Amorth, 21.

who truly saves is God and He alone. Part of his instrumentality is obeying the command of Jesus. Therefore, "Jesus said that 'this kind [of demon] can only come out through prayer and fasting.' For this, mindful of these words, the exorcist must strive to make use of these two very powerful tools to implore divine help and expel demons."[67] As he would later write, in order to drive out the devil, "much faith, much prayer, and fasting are always needed: on part of both those who intercede, and those for whom we intercede."[68] Thus, prayer and fasting are part of the twenty-one rules for the exorcist he took to heart. The possessed must also do his part. As Father Amorth explained:

> The possessed must pray to their benefit if physically and mentally able. They must fast, go to confession, and receive communion for their support, according to the advice of the priest. And while they are being exorcised, they must be recollected. They must turn to God with firm faith and ask for health with all humility. And when they are more tormented by the devil, they must bear it with patience and never doubt God's help. The possessed must hold a crucifix in their hands, or in any case it should be within sight, or relics of the saints when they are available.[69]

These objects should be handled with the utmost caution so as not to expose them to the risk of demonic contamination.

The twenty-one rules, with few words and pointed questions, also give precise instructions about the behavior

---

67 Amorth, 21.
68 Amorth, *An Exorcist Tells*, 153.
69 Amorth, *L'Ultimo Esorcista*, 22.

of the exorcist. For example, "[The exorcist] must command the unclean spirit to be silent and respond only to his questions."[70] He should not allow the unclean spirit to mislead by giving false answers, such as being the soul of a saint or a deceased person or an angel. An adroit and cunning predator, the devil likes to lie and play hide-and-seek with his exorcist enemies.

There are also questions that must be asked according to the Rite. Father Amorth lists them: the exorcist "must ask the devil: 'What is your name? Are you alone or are you many? When did you enter this person? Why did you decide to possess this person?'"[71] It is necessary, he explains, to know who is being dealt with, to look him in the face, and call evil by its name. Thus, the lies are exposed and the devil is forced to present himself for what he is and to pronounce his own name. Father Amorth added, "As for the other futilities of the devil—laughter, swear words, insults, objects he inexplicably spits out of the mouth of the possessed, trifles—the exorcist must cut them off, or in any case scorn them. He should also admonish his collaborators [assistant-priests and lay associates], who must be few and well-prepared, not to pay attention to him and not ask the possessed any questions, but rather to pray to God for him or her with humility and determination."[72]

The exorcist must not be weak with Satan. On the contrary, he must confront him authoritatively, without indulging him or being timid. He must be armed with faith, humility, and conviction. He should always have the customary holy water at hand, ready to sprinkle on the possessed at any time, to counteract the attacks—including

70   Amorth, 22.
71   Amorth, 22–23.
72   Amorth, 23.

physical—by the evil one. He should repeat, "even to the point of exhaustion," says Father Amorth, those words that most annoy the demons. This counterattack can last for hours. The exorcist should not offer medicine or [medical] treatment to the possessed, because the demon can feign sickness in an attempt to end the session. He leaves this up to a doctor. The exorcist works only with the word, preferably that of the Bible, prayers, the crucifix, and holy water.

The unclean spirit will try every tactic to stop the prayer sessions, including creating scandal. Thus, when praying for a woman, explained Father Amorth, "a trusted person should always be present, to hold the possessed woman tightly while she is being agitated by the devil. If possible, there should be family members." He should stick to the ritual and "be on guard not to say or do anything that could be an occasion for bad thoughts for him, her, or for others present."[73] Finally, he explains how the exorcist should command the devil to

> say if he entered that body as a result of sorcery or cursed signs or something cursed that the possessed had eaten. In the latter case, the possessed should vomit it out. If, on the other hand, he used things external to the person, he should say where they are and, after finding them, they should be burned. The possessed person should be admonished to reveal to the exorcist any temptations he or she may have. If the possessed were to be freed at that point, he or she should be carefully admonished to beware of sin so as not to offer the devil the opportunity to return.

---

73   Amorth, 23.

In this case, the condition could become worse than before the deliverance.[74]

This echoes the words of Jesus who said to those whom He had healed from evil of body or spirit, "Go and sin no more" (Jn 8:11). Thus does the exorcist to pronounce those same clear and definitive words, because sin is the vehicle of the devil.

Twenty-one rules of engagement. Father Amorth put to memory these general rules, written in Latin and valid and binding for all exorcists. Father Amorth said, regarding them, "Fr. Candido asked me to learn them by heart before I began to exorcise. These are fundamental rules, even if, during the battle, anything can happen." Like any battle, however, a general must be able to improvise and adapt according to the enemy's stratagems. When in doubt, however, call in the Blessed Mother for help. As Father Amorth recalls, "Sometimes what has been studied is of little use. Or almost no use. In these cases, there is one thing that needs to be done: invoke the help of a special person. I cannot say how many times Our Lady has come to my aid. She has been at my side since my first exorcism—even before, always, throughout my life."[75]

Marian consecration was the secret to the success of the Mariologist (*mariologo*) who was, in fact, a thief (*mariuolo*) who stole many souls back for God. Father Amorth was consecrated to Our Lady by Father Alberione during the war. He was clothed in the invisible, impenetrable protective shield that his mother had asked for him from the founder of the Paulines. With her protection, he faced the

---

[74]   Amorth, 23–24.
[75]   Amorth, 24.

devil. Every time he pronounced the name of Mary, the enemy trembled. That shield was his additional weapon, the secret weapon that allowed Father Amorth to go to battle without fear:

> Every time I perform an exorcism, I go to battle. Before beginning, I wear a breastplate: a purple stole whose length is longer than those usually worn by priests when we say Mass. I often wrap the stole around the shoulders of the possessed. This is effective. It serves to calm the possessed when they go into a trance during the exorcism and drool, scream, acquire superhuman strength, and attack. I take with me the book in Latin with the exorcism formulas and holy water, which I sometimes sprinkle on the possessed person, and also a crucifix embedded with a medal of Saint Benedict. This is a special medal, much feared by Satan.[76]

The exorcist's task is not pleasant. Nor is his a fascinating, adventurous, or exciting job. It involves fighting on the front line, face-to-face with the enemy. Perhaps this is the reason why there are so few of them. Few priests today take to heart the command of Jesus to the apostles to "cast out demons" (Mt 10:8). This is, perhaps, the most serious of all the missions assigned by Jesus to His bishops and priests. If preaching, celebrating the Mass, witnessing, evangelizing, and administering the sacraments are *preventive* actions, exorcism is the *repressive* practice of evil. It involves freeing people, eradicating from the body the enemy who has fraudulently taken possession of and seized his victim with the goal separating him from God for all eternity. We know

---

[76]   Amorth, 27.

that the evil one does not intend to let go of his conquest, of his claim to victory over God. Therefore, he reacts with violence, anger, and arrogance. He unleashes fierce attacks, which are humanly impossible to resist without superior aid and firepower.

The exorcist, therefore, must be patient. Father Amorth said to Paolo Rodari, "The battle can last for hours. And it almost never ends with deliverance. It takes years to free a possessed person. Many years. Satan is difficult to defeat. Often he hides, and he remains hidden. He does his best not to be found. The exorcist's job is to find him. He must force him to say his name. And then, in the name of Christ, the exorcist must force him to leave."[77]

The devil resists with every means at his disposal. Collaborators [lay-associates] are required to keep the possessed person still. They must remain in silence, however, for if they speak, Satan often attacks them directly. Only the exorcist must speak. Notably, his speech should not be dialogue because this can easily be manipulated by the evil one, who is stronger in words than any human being. The exorcist only gives orders in the name of God and according to the Rite. They are dry, peremptory orders, which leave no room for doubt. This is the only converse necessary.

Father Amorth would exorcise frequently each day, performing as many as ten to twelve in twenty-four-hour periods. He would work every day, "even on Sundays, even Christmas." For this, his teacher, Father Candido, reproached him: "You must take some days off. You cannot always exorcise." But these were words to the wind. He would continue at a fast pace, without resting, even at the risk of his own health. He would not stop. He

---

77   Amorth, 27.

encountered thousands upon thousands of people. The battle was a lengthy, tense, and exhausting war against the enemy of man.

Father Amorth admitted that although he had become an expert in the task of exorcism, it was still not easy to face the devil. He recalls his very first exorcism. "The difficulties I encounter today," he once admitted, "are the same as those I encountered the first time. After months of practicing exorcisms alone at home, Father Candido said to me, 'Have courage, today it's your turn. Today you enter into battle.'"

It was his first exorcism. A few months after receiving the mandate from Cardinal Poletti, it was his turn. A case was brought to Father Candido by a Franciscan friar named Father Massimiliano who had Croatian roots. He knew of a farmer who was likely possessed. Father Candido did not have time, so he sent Father Amorth. Father Amorth remembers his doubts. He asked Father Candido, "Are you really sure I am ready?" His mentor pointedly replied, "No one is ever ready for this kind of thing. But you are sufficiently prepared to begin. Remember that each battle has its risks. You will have to encounter them one at a time." It was, in a sense, spiritual "last rites," or viaticum without appeal. That day remained forever etched in the exorcist's memory: February 21, 1987.

The appointment was set for a discreet room in the Antonianum in Via Merulana, not far from Saint John in Lateran where he first prayed for the strength to perform his new assigned task. Father Amorth arrived early for the appointment with some trepidation. He had practiced assiduously and was well prepared, but this time it was real. He did not even know the case well. Who would show up? What was about to happen in that room?

Father Massimiliano entered followed by a young man, about twenty-five years old. He had the air of a country person. Then an unknown third man entered unexpectedly, introducing himself as the translator. Father Amorth was surprised, as there could be no one else present. He knew it was potentially dangerous because Satan could attack anyone present. Father Massimiliano reassured him and explained that when he goes into a trance [a diabolic manifestation often begins with a trance-like state], the young man spoke in English, and someone had to translate into Italian. The translator was prepared for the assignment and would be careful.

With journalistic passion and precision, Father Amorth recounted in detail his first exorcism to Paolo Rodari:

I wear my stole, I take the breviary and the crucifix in my hand. I have holy water close at hand. I begin to recite the exorcism in Latin.

"Do not remind yourself, Lord, of our sins or that of our parents and do not punish us for our sins. Our Father ... And lead us not into temptation, but deliver us from evil."

The possessed is like a pillar of salt. He does not speak. He does not react. He remains motionless sitting on the wooden chair where I had him sit. I recite Psalm 54: "O God, by your name save me. By your strength defend my cause. O God, hear my prayer. Listen to the words of my mouth. Strangers have risen against me; the ruthless seek my life; they do not keep God before them."

Still there is no reaction. The farmer is silent, his gaze fixed on the ground.

"God is present as my helper; the Lord sustains my life. Turn back the evil upon my foes; in your faithfulness, destroy them. Then I will offer you generous sacrifice and give thanks to your name, LORD, for it is good. Because it has rescued me from every trouble, and my eyes look down on my foes. Glory to the Father . . ."

"Save your servant who trusts in you, my God. Let him find in you, Lord, a fortified tower. In the face of the enemy, let the enemy have no power over him. And the son of iniquity be powerless to harm him Lord. Send him aid from your holy place. And watch over him from Sion. Lord, heed my prayer. And let my cry be heard by you. The Lord be with you. May He also be with you."

At this point, the farmer raises his head suddenly and stares at me. In the same instant, he explodes in an angry, frightening scream. He turns red and starts screaming invectives in English. He remains seated. He doesn't come close to me. He seems to fear me. But he wants to scare me.

"Priest, stop it! Shut up, shut up, shut up!"

He lashes out with curses, swear words, and threats. I speed up the ritual.

"Holy Lord, almighty Father, everlasting God and Father of our Lord Jesus Christ, who once and for all consigned that fallen and apostate tyrant to the flames of hell, who sent your only-begotten Son into the world to crush that roaring lion; hasten to our call for help and snatch from ruination and from the clutches of the noonday devil this human being made in your image and likeness. Strike terror, Lord, into the beast now laying waste your vineyard. Fill your servants with courage to fight manfully against that reprobate dragon, lest he despise those who put their trust in you, and say with Pharaoh of old: 'I know not God, nor will I set Israel free.' Let your mighty hand cast him out of your servant, so he may no longer hold captive this person whom it pleased you to make in your image, and to redeem through your Son; who lives and reigns with you, in the unity of the Holy Spirit, God, forever and ever."

The possessed man continues to scream in English: "Shut up, shut up, shut up!" He spits on the ground and on me. He is furious. He's like a lion about to pounce. It is evident that his prey is me. I understand that I have to go on. And I arrive up to the *Praecipio tibi* (I command you).

I remember well what Father Candido told me when he instructed me on the tricks of the trade: "Always remember that the *Praecipio tibi* is often the resolution prayer. Remember that it is the prayer most feared by demons. I really believe it is the most effective. When the going gets tough, when the devil is furious and seems strong and unassailable, go there quickly. You will benefit from it in battle. You will see how effective that prayer is. Recite it aloud and with authority. Throw it at the possessed. You will see the effects."

I say, "I command you, unclean spirit, whoever you are, along with all your minions now attacking this servant of God, by the mysteries of the incarnation, passion, resurrection, and ascension of our Lord Jesus Christ, by the descent of the Holy Spirit, by the coming of our Lord for judgment, that you tell me by some sign your name, and the day and hour of your departure. I command you, moreover, to obey me to the letter, I who am a minister of God despite my unworthiness; nor shall you be emboldened to harm in any way this creature of God, or the bystanders, or any of their possessions."

The possessed continues to scream. Now his moan becomes a cry and seems to come from the recesses of the earth. I insist, "Therefore, I adjure you every unclean spirit, every specter from hell, every satanic power, in the name of Jesus Christ, to uproot you and flee from this creature of God."

The scream becomes a howl. And it gets stronger and stronger. It seems infinite.

"Hearken, therefore, and tremble in fear, Satan, you enemy of the faith, you foe of the human race, you begetter of death, you robber of life, you corrupter of justice, you root of all evil and vice; seducer of men, betrayer of the nations, instigator of envy, font of avarice, fomenter of discord, author of pain and sorrow."

His eyes roll backwards. His head hangs behind the back of the chair. The scream continues in a frightening high pitch. Father Massimiliano tries to keep him still while the translator takes a few steps back in fear. I wave him back farther. Satan is unleashed.

"Why, then, do you stand and resist, knowing as you must that Christ the Lord brings your plans to nothing? Fear Him, who in Isaac was offered in sacrifice, in Joseph sold into bondage, slain as the paschal lamb, crucified as man, yet triumphed over the powers of hell. Begone, then, in the name of the Father, and of the Son, and of the Holy Spirit."

The devil does not want to give up. But then his cry suddenly fades and he looks at me. A little bit of drool comes out of his mouth. I pursue him. I know I have to force him to reveal himself, to tell me his name. If he tells me his name, it is a sign that he is almost defeated. By revealing himself, in fact, I force him to reveal his cards.

"And now tell me, unclean spirit, who are you? Tell me your name! Tell me, in the name of Jesus Christ, your name!"

This is the first time I have done a serious exorcism and is, thus, the first time I ask a demon to reveal his name to me. His answer chills me.

"I am Lucifer," he says [in English] in a low voice, slowly pronouncing all the syllables. "I am Lucifer."

I must not give up. I mustn't give up now. I must not be scared. I must continue the exorcism with authority. I am leading the game. Not him.

"I adjure you, ancient serpent, by the judge of the living and the dead, by your Creator, by the Creator of the whole universe, by Him who has the power to consign you to hell, to depart forthwith in fear, along with your savage minions, from this servant of God, who seeks refuge in the fold of the Church. I adjure you again, not by my weakness but by the might of the Holy Spirit, to depart from this servant of God, whom almighty God has made in His image. Yield, therefore, yield not to my own person but to the minister of Christ. For it is the power of Christ that compels you, who brought you low by His cross. Tremble before that mighty arm that broke asunder the dark prison walls and led souls forth to light."

The possessed starts to howl again. His head is thrown back again behind the back of the chair. His back is curved. More than an hour has passed.

Father Candido always told me, "As long as you have energy and strength, continue. You mustn't give up. An exorcism can last up to a day. Give in only when you realize you cannot hold up physically." I think back on everything Father Candido said to me. I wish he were here next to me. But he is not. I have to do it alone.

"May the trembling that afflicts this human frame, the fear that afflicts this image of God, descend on you. Make no resistance nor delay in departing from this man, for it has pleased Christ to dwell in man. Do not think of despising my command because you know me to be a great sinner. It is God Himself who commands you; the majestic Christ who commands you. God the Father commands you; God the Son commands you; God the Holy Spirit commands you. The mystery of the cross commands you."

Before I began, I didn't think that such a thing could happen. But suddenly I have the distinct sensation of a demonic presence in front of me. I feel this devil staring at me. He scrutinizes me. He goes around me. The air becomes cold, terribly cold. Father Candido had warned me of sudden changes in temperature. It is one thing to hear about certain things, but another to experience them. I try to concentrate. I close my eyes and continue my supplication from memory.

"Depart, then, transgressor. Depart, seducer, full of lies and cunning, foe of virtue, persecutor of the innocent. Give place, abominable creature, give way, you monster, give way to Christ, in whom you found none of your works. For He has already stripped you of your powers and laid waste your kingdom, bound you prisoner and plundered your weapons. He has cast you forth into the outer darkness, where everlasting ruin awaits you and your abettors. To what purpose do you insolently resist? To what purpose do you brazenly refuse? For you are guilty before almighty God, whose laws you have transgressed. You are guilty before His Son, our Lord Jesus Christ, whom you presumed to tempt, whom you dared to nail to the cross. You are guilty before the whole human race, to whom you proffered by your enticements the poisoned cup of death."

At this point, something unexpected occurs. It was an event that would never happen again in the course of my long career as an exorcist. The possessed becomes like a piece of wood. His legs go forward. His head is stretched back. He starts to levitate. He rises horizontally half a meter above the back of the chair. For several minutes, he remains there motionless, suspended in the air. Father Massimiliano takes a step back. I remain in my place with the crucifix tightly in my right hand, the ritual in the other. I remember the stole. I take it and touch the body of the possessed with the end. He remains still, motionless. Stiff. Silent. I strike another blow.

"Depart, then, impious one, depart, accursed one, depart with all your deceits, for God has willed that man should be His temple. Why do you still linger here? Give honor to God the Father Almighty, before whom every knee must bow. Give place to the Lord Jesus Christ, who shed His most Precious Blood for man. Give place to the Holy Spirit, who by His blessed apostle Peter openly struck you down in the person of Simon Magus; who cursed your lies in Annas and

Saphira; who smote you in King Herod because he had not given honor to God; who by His apostle Paul afflicted you with the night of blindness in the magician Elyma, and by the mouth of the same apostle bade you to go out of Pythonissa, the soothsayer. Begone, now! Begone, seducer! Your place is in solitude; your abode is in the nest of serpents; get down and crawl with them. This matter brooks no delay; for see, the Lord, the ruler comes quickly, kindling fire before Him, and it will run on ahead of Him and encompass His enemies in flames. You might delude man, but God you cannot mock. It is He who casts you out, from whose sight nothing is hidden. It is He who repels you, to whose might all things are subject. It is He who expels you, He who has prepared everlasting hellfire for you and your angels, from whose mouth shall come a sharp sword, who is coming to judge both the living and the dead and the world by fire. Amen."

A thud accompanies my *Amen*. The possessed man collapses in his chair. He sputters words that I struggle to understand. Then he says in English, "I'll be out on 21 June at 3:00 p.m. I'll be out on 21 June at 3:00 p.m."

Then he looks at me. Now his eyes are those of the poor farmer. They are full of tears. I realize that he has come back to his senses. I embrace him and tell him, "It will end soon."

I decided to repeat the exorcism each week. The same thing happens every time. On the week of 21 June, I left him alone. I did not want to interfere with the day Lucifer said he would be leaving. I know I shouldn't trust him, but sometimes the devil is unable to lie.

The week following that of 21 June, I called him to come back again. He arrives as always accompanied by Father Massimiliano and the translator. He seems serene. I begin to exorcise him. There is no reaction. He remains calm, clear, and serene. I sprinkle some holy water on him. Still there is no reaction. I ask him to recite the Ave Maria with me. He says it without going into a rage. I ask him to tell me what happened on the day Lucifer said he was going to leave him.

He said, "As I do every day, I went to work in the fields alone. In the early afternoon, I decided to take a ride on the tractor. At 3:00 p.m., I felt like screaming very loud. I think I bellowed out a terrifying scream. At the end of the scream, I felt free. I don't know how to explain it. I was free."

Never again did I experience a similar case. I would never be so fortunate again to free a possessed person in so few sessions, in just four months. It was a miracle. Subsequent exorcisms last for years. I do not know why my first exorcism went so smoothly. It was terrifying, but easy. Nor do I know why it was the only time I ever witnessed levitation. I really do not know what God was trying to say to me. Perhaps He wanted me to experience all of Satan's wickedness but also to give me courage—to show me I could do it. I talked about it at length with Father Candido, who, on the other hand, gave me a completely different interpretation.[78]

---

[78] Amorth, 29–37.

10

"I HAVE NEVER BEEN AFRAID"

"You're wrong to ask yourself so many questions," Father Candido said. Father Amorth was trying to understand why his first exorcism was such a success. He wanted to know why it went so quickly and what God was trying to tell him. Father Candido's response deflated his enthusiasm: "It is not God who was speaking to you, but Satan. Never ask yourself if God is behind an exorcism. Certainly, it is God who defeats Satan. He is victorious through the exorcism. But do not ask yourself things that no one can answer. Do not commit the sin of pride. Do what you must and do not ask too many questions. Don't you know that we are merely useless servants?"[79]

It was a lesson of humility received and accepted: do not ask too many questions; do not become prideful; God defeats Satan, and definitely not man. He would later recall his experience for other priests: "I will continue to repeat this—and I beg you to believe me: the devil is already

---

[79]   Amorth, *L'Ultimo Esorcista*, 37.

causing each one of us as much harm as he's allowed to do. It is false to believe that if I leave him alone, he will leave me alone. It is not only false; it is also a betrayal of our priestly ministry, which should be directed solely at leading souls to God, even by removing them from Satan's power, if necessary."

Thus, he learned from Father Candido the need for a priest not to be afraid of the devil. "A priest who is afraid of the devil's reprisal," Father Amorth insists, "can be compared to a shepherd who is afraid of the wolf. It is a groundless fear." A priest is to boldly evangelize and preach the power and primacy of the sacraments, and the use of holy water and other "sacramentals, and exorcism among them."[80]

Exorcism, then, is a sacramental to be used by priests as part of his normal duties. In addition to holy water, Father used a long purple stole, and the Saint Benedict medal, there was something else Father Candido suggested Father Amorth always bring to exorcisms: a special oil. "You get it by mixing together the oil of catechumens used at baptisms and the oil of the sick. Always sign the possessed on his or her forehead, then in the senses—eyes, ears, nostrils, mouth, and throat. Then say the ritual prayer. If you are able, learn it by heart so you don't have to keep the book in your pocket."[81]

He received many valuable suggestions from Father Candido, who witnessed all kinds of things in his decades against Satan. His mentor told Father Amorth:

Stay very close to the possessed. If you can, keep your hand on his or her head. Make the sign of the cross on them often. Remember this prayer of deliverance I

[80]   Amorth, *An Exorcist Tells*, 194.
[81]   Amorth, *L'Ultimo Esorcista*, 38.

learned from a nun, Sr. Erminia Brunetti, a Daughter of St. Paul, who died in the odor of sanctity. It is very effective: "Spirit of the Lord, Spirit of God, Father, Son, Holy Spirit, Holy Trinity, Immaculate Virgin, angels, archangels, saints of heaven come down on this person, melt him Lord, mold him, fill him with you, use him, drive away from him all the forces of evil, annihilate them, destroy them so that he can be well, do good, cast away from him all curses, witchcraft, black magic, black masses, hexes, bindings, maledictions, evil eyes, diabolical infestation, diabolic possession, diabolic obsession, all that is evil, sin, envy, jealousy, perfidy, illnesses that are physical, psychic, moral, spiritual, and diabolic. Burn all these evils in hell so that they never again have to touch him or any other creature in the world. I order and command with the power of Almighty God in the name of Jesus Christ the Savior, through the intercession of the Immaculate Virgin, with the power I have from the Church, although unworthy, to all unclean spirits, to all presences that molest him, to leave him immediately, to leave him permanently and to go to eternal hell chained by St. Michael the Archangel, by St. Gabriel, by St. Raphael, by our guardian angels, crushed under the heel of the most holy Virgin Mary. Amen."

Watch how the damned react after hearing this prayer! They go wild.[82]

He added:

Do not be frightened if the possessed react strangely at the beginning of the exorcism. Do not be struck by

---

[82]   Amorth, 38–39.

their sobbing, angry movements, or spitting. Let them throw themselves on the ground, let them writhe like snakes. If you can, get help from assistants to keep them still. Once the exorcism has begun, interrogate the devil. The interrogation is important. Never ask trivial questions, only questions useful for deliverance. The first question should be: "What is your name?" The devil does everything he can to hide. Revealing his name is a huge undertaking because it means he has to unveil himself. But he must say it, because he cannot resist the power of exorcism. "When did you enter? How did you get in? What do you intend to do with this person? When will you leave?" These are the main questions. If the devil doesn't answer, repeat these questions until he does.

But remember that the devil lies. His answers must always be checked.

I once had a very difficult case. There was a girl I couldn't free. I asked the devil: "When will you leave her?" To which he replied: "On 8 December." This is a significant date, the feast of the Immaculate Conception. Then, when 8 December arrived, I called her and did a long exorcism, but she still hadn't broken free. After five and a half hours of exorcism, she finally seemed free. She jumped for joy with tears of happiness. She really seemed free. After a week, however, she was the same as before. I asked the devil: "Why didn't you leave? You said you were leaving on 8 December, why didn't you go away?" With a scornful voice, he said: "Didn't they ever tell you that I'm a liar? Didn't they teach you that I lie?"

Why does the Lord allow certain things? It is difficult if not impossible to answer these questions.

We look very much at this world, while God looks very much at eternity. Therefore, it is probable that he allows possession to obtain some advantage for souls that is valid for eternity.[83]

Many are the traps of Satan. Father Candido warned the new exorcist of the snares of this terrible and powerful enemy—one that is shrewd and unscrupulous. It would be an extraordinary battle, one not to be taken lightly or superficially, nor with the presumption of being victorious with little effort. Woe to assume too much from one's own strength.

Father Candido admonished:

Do not think that it is easy to free someone who is possessed. The time frames are always very long. You are fighting against absolute evil, blind evil. It will not be a walk in the park. The evil one is pure spirit. He is a force that enters the body. But sometimes it can simply be a spirit acting on a person without possessing him. Be careful not to believe that everyone is possessed. Many simply have a negative influence perhaps caused by a curse, but are not possessed. Padre Pio of Pietrelcina, for example, suffered attacks from the devil every day, with rare exceptions. He was beaten, knocked to the ground. These are vexations, but he was not possessed. So, too, was the Curé of Ars, John Marie Vianney. They suffered very serious vexation, but not possession.[84]

---

[83] Amorth, 39–40.

[84] By vexations is meant spiritual oppression, or a form of extraordinary diabolic influence in which a demon attacks a person externally. God often allows vexations for the person to grow in sanctity

Others suffer damage to their homes—creaks,
pops, lights that go on and off randomly or burst. I
knew an engineer who had thirty to forty light bulbs
a month burst at his home. These phenomena are
cured with exorcisms. But there is no possession. It is
possible that these houses had been inhabited in the
past by a sorcerer who performed séances or someone who performed satanic rites. Or it is possible that
the house was built over a former cemetery. I repeat,
these are not possessions, but can still be difficult
cases. You can do exorcisms if you want, but remember that you do not have the devil himself before you
[in these cases]. Exorcisms, in fact, can be carried out
on possessed persons but also on *res*, on things; that
is, on houses, objects, or animals.[85]

It seems like it is an uneven match. And it is, at the
human level. No man alone can hunt down and defeat the
devil. His strength is such and so great that not even an
army could bring him down. The exorcist is an instrument
in the hands of God. He acts on behalf of God, and he fights
the good fight of God. Alone he can do nothing—against
the enemy with a thousand weapons and with many diabolical inventions.

Father Candido continued to guide Father Amorth's
initial steps:

Often Satan is not alone in the bodies of the people he
possesses. Sometimes there are many demons. Jesus
often speaks of legions. Once, I was exorcising a nun.

and to glorify God by defeating the devil.
[85]   Amorth, *L'Ultimo Esorcista*, 40.

There was a tremendous amount of possession. She was vomiting everything.

"How many are you?" I asked.

"Legions, legions, legions," they responded. While I exorcised her, she was constantly squirming. And she jumped from wall to wall like a monkey. It was impossible to keep her still.[86]

Father Candido also warned against Satan's disguises. Being dispossessed of a human body, he can take the form of different people, depending on who is before him. "To Padre Pio," he explained, "the devil presented himself in the form of Jesus, sometimes as Mary, sometimes as his superior, or sometimes as his confessor."[87]

He learned from his teacher the necessity to adjust one's method, even if it must always be adapted to the specific case, to the man or woman who is possessed or presumed as such. The devil's weakness must be discovered and attacked. Father Candido explained to Father Amorth, "One exorcist by naming Padre Pio can provoke a strong reaction in the possessed, while another exorcist in naming him may not have any effect whatsoever. You have to find your own way. It will be your way. Always remember Saint Leopold Mandic. He lived in Padua. He heard confessions all day long. Often exorcists called on him for help. He would arrive, attend the exorcism in silence, and then would intervene at the end, saying, 'Out, out. Go away.' And the spellbound devil would disappear. That was his way. You, too, must find yours."[88]

---

[86]   Amorth, 41.
[87]   Amorth, 41.
[88]   Amorth, 41.

In addition, Father Candido warned his protégé that he must not enter into dialogue with the devil. There should be no debates or negotiations. He is the enemy, not any human adversary. He must be fought, he must be driven out, he must be defeated. Therefore, Father Candido insisted, "It is he who must answer your questions and not you his. Whoever participates in an exorcism must not speak with the devil. Only exorcists can do so, because they are the only ones protected."

There is also fear to deal with, which should not be overlooked. Satan has many ways to frighten his enemies and make them feel unsafe. Father Candido knew this well and warned his disciple:

> The devil will threaten you. He often causes noises in my room at night. Do not fear. If you are with God, it is he who is afraid of you. Exorcism is a battle. It is a struggle. There is much tension. You have to bring a tremendous amount of inner strength. Strength must come from within. You must act with the spirit more than with the body. Concentrate. Pray. It takes faith, for God rewards faith. Recall the Gospel: "Go, your faith has saved you" (Lk 17:19). Do not think that God or Our Lady will speak to you, that they will suggest what you should do. Consider, rather, that they are with you, and there is also a person with you who will never leave you—your guardian angel.[89]

Regarding the fear of Satan, Father Amorth stated to Elisabetta Fezzi:

> I have never been afraid, not even at the beginning! Never! I always say that it is the devil who is afraid

---

[89]   Amorth, 42.

of me. I have said several times on television: "When
the devil sees me, he poops his pants!" In the beginning, I was with Father Candido, who had my back.
Then I made an iron pact with Our Lady! The devil
told me many times: "We cannot do anything to you,
because you are too protected." I have my guardian
angel, I have Saint Gabriel, my namesake, and I have
the mantle of the Madonna! I feel like a nobleman,
always safe! I have a lot of help from up there, but the
ones just mentioned are the foundation. Wrapped in
Mary's mantle, I have no fear. I never even had trou-
bles, while Father Candido did. Father Candido was
a Passionist and worked at the Holy Stairs. Once, he
was away from Rome and one of his confreres arrived
unannounced. So they put him up in his room. The
next day, Father Candido returned and his brother
priest asked him: "How can you sleep in this room?
There are constant noises, constant noises." He
replied: "I don't mind!" He would arise every night
and go to the chapel for an hour of Adoration. Father
Candido was a man of great prayer! I found out from
someone who was aiding him that he was attacked
by the devil in his final moments: he stiffened and
became serious and severe. [90]

With that, Father Amorth went to battle with Satan.
He learned the basics of exorcism and grew in his abilities. Father Amorth knew and recognized that he owed
very much to Father Candido, from whom learned everything. He referred to him as his teacher. He guided him
at the beginning of his new and tortuous journey, full of
unknown and frightening pitfalls and stumbling blocks. He

---

[90]   Fezzi, *La Mia Battaglia Contro Satana*, 50–51.

gave him the physical and spiritual tools to face the enemy. He encouraged and supported him in the beginning.

His experiences gradually gave him the tools to refine his apostolate on the front line. He explained that there are six stages that every exorcism passes through. The first is to sense the demonic presence. The devil is not seen, but he is there. He acts. Therefore, "it is necessary to remain calm and have a lot of faith. To find within yourself the proper strength to react, to fight back, to make this presence sense who is in charge, who is leading the game." The second step is to bring him out into the open, to force him to reveal himself with his name: "The name is important," explained Father Amorth, "because it says a lot about who is before you. For example, if a devil has a biblical name—Satan, Asmodeus, Beelzebub, Baal, Lucifer, or whatever—he is more powerful. There is a hierarchy in hell. Demons are also more important depending on the name they bear."[91] In this stage, the demon utilizes many tricks to obfuscate. He hides, he seeks to deceive the exorcist, he sometimes speaks with the voice of the possessed, and he sometimes remains calm. "Overcoming his pretenses and forcing the devil to speak is a feat that takes weeks, sometimes months. If the exorcist fails to make the devil reveal himself, he has lost."[92] When this happens, Father Amorth suggests it is better for him to step aside.

The third stage is the so-called breaking point. In identifying himself with his name, he no longer has any reason to hide. He therefore reveals himself in all his power and violence in a flood of screams, swear words, and insults. His voice changes and takes on inhuman tones. According

[91]   Amorth, *L'Ultimo Esorcista*, 43.
[92]   Amorth, 43.

to Father Amorth, "It is as if all the hatred present suddenly reveals itself in the body of the possessed."[93] This opens the case to the critical fourth stage. "At this moment," he says, "the exorcist must impose his authority. He must take the initiative and impose silence on the devil. In the name of Jesus and with the authority conferred on him by Jesus and His Church, the exorcist must silence the devil and take the lead in the battle."[94]

The fifth phase is the clash, or battle phase. This is the most terrible moment. The exorcist must attack hard. He must pursue the enemy and attack him with questions: "When will you go? Why have you entered? Who are you exactly? What do you want? Why are you harming this person?" With each response, his resistance will weaken. This is the point of no return, the moment of expulsion, the victory of the exorcist, and the deliverance of the possessed. Sometimes, the fifth stage is a very long path, as we have seen, because the devil resists as much as possible.

He does not want to leave that body he has conquered and subjugated. Eventually, the demon does abandon his house. Over time, the power and authority of Christ, through the prayers of the exorcist, overpowers the demon, giving way to the sixth stage. Father Amorth explains why the demon resists so fiercely:

It is very simple. Because he doesn't know where to go. Recall the Gospel when the unclean spirits ask Jesus: "Where should we go? We, too, must have a home." The body of the possessed is like a home that the unclean spirit has claimed. It is a house he does

---

[93]   Amorth, 44.
[94]   Amorth, 44.

not want to vacate. But he must abandon this house sooner or later, if only on the day when the possessed person dies.

The attempt of the exorcist is to cast him out before the possessed dies. For this reason—realizing that he must leave soon—the devil's response against the exorcist is ferocious. Often there is a nauseating smell in the room. There is a feeling of infinite anguish that pervades everything and everyone. It is as if the pure essence of evil is there. Evil and all that is anti-human are there. Two worlds face off— the world of good against the world of evil. There are two worlds that correspond to two possibilities. If the exorcist holds firm and clings to Christ, he reaches his final goal, the sixth, which is expulsion. Suddenly, the presence of the curse disappears. It is no more. Peace reigns. The possessed often remembers nothing. He feels free and happy.[95]

The school of exorcism brought a remarkable depth of knowledge to Father Gabriele Amorth. He was, in fact, an exorcist by chance—even if "chance" for believers is according to the inscrutable design of God and His will since before the world existed and in accordance with His inexhaustible creativity. In God's inscrutable design, he would fight against the devil for thirty years. This was an extraordinarily long time, considering the battle is so physically and spiritually exhausting. Despite the fatigue, disappointments, and losses, the former Resistance fighter would never retreat from the enemy. The devil and his hosts of legions were confronted by a most stubborn and difficult

---

[95]   Amorth, 45.

adversary. This daily struggle for the triumph of good over evil ended only at the end of his earthly life.

He fought countless times with the devil who appeared under various titles and forms. As Father Amorth recalls, this was "sometimes Satan, other times a more or less important servant, or sometimes several of his servants. There are many exorcisms that I can talk about. I remember many in detail."[96] How can one forget the struggle with the devil, with the enemy of God and man? Father Amorth freed many brothers and sisters from the power of the evil one. In truth, he fought the battle that others did not want to face—out of laziness, bad faith, or fear. Or for little faith.

---

[96]   Amorth, 45.

11

HIS EMINENCE DOES NOT BELIEVE IN SATAN

An exorcism is a descent into the lower circles of hell, a battle face-to-face with demons. It is ostensibly an uneven match. As such, organization is urgently needed. The (few) exorcists out there need to get together, team up, and meet. They need to get to know each other, exchange experiences, and encourage one another. Against the legions of devils, a small army of men devoted to battling them must get organized. At least Father Amorth believed so.

About five years after receiving his assignment from Cardinal Poletti, in 1991, he founded the National [Italian] Association of Exorcists. Three years later, it was opened to the world, becoming known as the International Association of Exorcists (IAE). It is the only organization of its kind recognized by the Church, having been approved by the Congregation for the Clergy in 2014. Father Amorth was its creator and would be its lifeblood. He presided over it until 2000, subsequently becoming honorary president until his death.

According to a 2019 census, there were 404 IAE exorcists in the world, in addition to 124 auxiliaries, or collaborators in various capacities. Of these, 240 are in Italy—by far the highest number. However, given that there are 225 dioceses in the country means that there is roughly one for each diocese, plus sixty-two auxiliaries. Poland has the second highest number, with 120 exorcists, though they are not members of the association. Then, in descending order: the United Kingdom has 28 exorcists and 4 auxiliaries; Spain has 15 plus 9; the Czech Republic-Slovakia has 9 plus 1. In the United States, there are only 21 exorcists, while Mexico has 15.[97] There are a few more scattered here and there who do not belong to the IAE, but their numbers are dramatically few. The point is that there are too few exorcists in the world. In many cases, bishops do not even consider the issue at all for their dioceses. And yet, phenomena of occultism and satanism, mysterious sects, sorcerers and healers of all kinds, gurus and dangerous charlatans are all on the rise. Due to the internet, their potentially devastating messages are only amplified.

Father Amorth managed to bring the work of exorcism to the attention of the Church and to educate bishops and cardinals. He convinced many of them to appoint exorcists, though there are still not as many as are needed. Too many have reservations. There is too much resistance and timidity. The devil has convinced many that he does not exist, and it is convenient to believe this is true. In a secularized, post-Christian world, mention of Satan and his followers all too easily can lead to accusations of medieval obscurantism.

---

[97] To date, there are approximately ninety mandated exorcists (those working in official capacity with canonical authority from their local ordinary) in the United States.

In his book written with Paolo Rodari, Father Amorth recounted a striking dialogue he had with a certain cardinal. It reveals the widespread belief and mentality that exists not just outside but, unfortunately, inside the Church. Here it is in full:

> "Good morning Eminence, I am Fr. Gabriele Amorth. I am a Pauline priest. I live in Rome. I am also the official exorcist of the . . ."
>
> "I know who you are. I've heard of you. Tell me. What do you want?"
>
> "I need to meet you."
>
> "For what reason?"
>
> "Well, you see, I've put together an association of exorcists. We meet in Rome to dialogue and help one another. You know, there are so few of us in the world."
>
> "Look. I don't have time now. If you want, you can come to my home tomorrow and tell me what you want. Good day."
>
> The cardinal hangs up the telephone rather abruptly. Or at least it seems that way to me. Something tells me he doesn't like me. I have an idea why, but I wish to meet him anyway.
>
> The next day I show up at his house at the appointed time. An obsequious priest enters a room at the end of a corridor. He comes out a few moments later without looking at me. He comes toward me, then enters another room without saying anything to me.
>
> "Come in!" shouts a hoarse voice from the room at the end of the corridor. I enter. His Eminence is seated in an armchair. The television is on in front

of him, the remote control in his hand. He gestures for me to sit in an armchair next to the TV. Once I sit down, he turns off the television.

"You wanted to see me. Here I am. What do you need?"

"So, Eminence, I wanted to inform you that, as an exorcist of the Diocese of Rome, I thought of convening a small gathering of exorcists. There are so few of us in the world and very few in Italy. I believe that gathering would benefit us. It is such a difficult job. So I have come here to inform you of this initiative."

"But you must inform Ruini (the vicar of Rome), not me. I run a Vatican office which, on paper, may have jurisdiction over the matter, but only on paper. The one who needs to be informed is Ruini."

"Your Eminence, Ruini is already informed. I have written to him personally. It seemed a good thing to alert you too."

"Yes, yes, for heaven's sake. You did the right thing. But this story of the devil?"

"Pardon me?"

"I'm saying . . . You're an exorcist, but we both know Satan does not exist, no?"

"What do you mean we know he doesn't exist?"

"Father Amorth, please. You know better than I that it's all superstition. Do you want to tell me that you really believe this?"

"Your Eminence, it amazes me to hear these words from such an important person as yourself."

"It surprises you? But how? Don't tell me you really believe it!"

"I believe that Satan exists."

"Really? Not me. And I hope nobody else believes it. Spreading certain fears is not a good thing."

"Well, Eminence, you don't have to tell me. In fact, if I can, I would like to suggest something."

"Tell me, then."

"You should read a book that might be able to help you."

"Oh yes? What book, Father Amorth?"

"You should read the Gospel."

An icy silence falls over the room. The cardinal looks at me with a serious mien without answering. So I pursue him.

"Eminence, it is the Gospel that speaks of the devil. It is the Gospel that tells of Jesus casting out demons. Not only that, it is the Gospel that says that among the powers Jesus gave to the apostles is that of casting out demons. What do you wish for me to do, throw the Gospel overboard?"

"No, but I . . ."

"Eminence, I wish to be frank with you. The Church commits a grave sin in not speaking of the devil anymore. The consequences of this attitude are very serious. Christ came and fought his battle. Against whom? Against Satan. And He was victorious. But he is still free to tempt the world. Today. Now. And what do you do? You are telling me that it is just superstition? So, is the Gospel also just superstitious? But how can the Church explain evil without speaking of the devil?"

"Father Amorth, it is true that Jesus cast out demons. But this is just an expression to highlight the power of Christ! The Gospel is a continuous expression of parables. They are all parables. Jesus always taught in parables."

"But Eminence, when Jesus wants to use a parable, He says so clearly. The Gospel says: 'Jesus told them this parable,' while the Gospel clearly distinguishes historical events that really happened: the healings, the teachings, the reproaches, the exorcisms, distinguishing the latter from the healings. When Jesus casts out demons, it is not a parable, but a reality. He did not fight a ghost, but a reality; otherwise it would have been a farce. Many saints fought with the devil, many saints were tempted by the devil. Think, for example, of the experiences of the desert fathers and how many saints performed exorcisms. So would they all be fake, all neurotic? How can you not believe in the existence of Satan?"

"Okay, but even if they were real facts, even if Jesus really did cast out demons, the fact remains that through His resurrection, Jesus conquered everything, and therefore also conquered the devil."

"Yes, that's true, He conquered everything. But this victory must be applied and must be embodied in the life of each of us. Christ has won, but His victory for us must be reaffirmed day after day. Our condition as men imposes this on us. The devil's action has not been completely annulled. The devil was not destroyed. The Gospel says that the devil exists and that he even tempted Christ. Jesus gave weapons. He gave them to us, too, to overcome him. The devil can still tempt us, we can all be tempted, as evidenced by the prayer against the evil one that Jesus Himself taught us—the Our Father. Until Vatican II, at the end of the Mass, prayers were said to Saint Michael the Archangel, the brief exorcism composed by Pope Leo XIII, and the Prologue of the Gospel of Saint John was read precisely as a means of deliverance." His Eminence no longer knew what to say. He does not speak and does not react. I get up, say goodbye, and leave. I think to myself that we have come to this point. Since before the Middle Ages, exorcists existed everywhere. Now, unfortunately, something changed.[98]

Yes, much has changed in humanity, in culture, and ultimately in the faith. At the end of the second millennium and the first decades of the third, Father Amorth admitted, "It seems Satan no longer exists. But this is not so. He exists . . . and how! Not believing in Satan is a very serious issue and one that leads to terrible consequences. It is a sin for which, unfortunately, many men of the Church are responsible."[99] Indeed, Satan has been victorious in convincing the world—and even many priests, bishops, and cardinals—of his nonexistence.

Father Amorth, in reality, fought a dual battle for thirty years: against Satan and against those who did not believe in Satan. "From the eighteenth century onwards," he noted, "the existence of the devil has been denied. Where does the fault lie? Certainly it is due to secularism, atheism preached to the masses, and rationalism from the scientific and cultural world. The consequences are in the loss of faith that we are still experiencing and, at the same time, in the growth of every form of superstition and in the expansion of every kind of occultism."[100]

---

[98]   Amorth, *L'Ultimo Esorcista*, 159–62.
[99]   Amorth, 169.
[100]   Amorth, 170.

Given all this, it would seem natural that the world would reject Satan and, with him, the very concept of evil, the idea of sin, and the prospect of hell. But the Catholic Church too? No. Because it rests on the Gospel. Satan is there, indeed, from the very beginning of Jesus's mission, from the temptation in the desert. How can the Church—with her bishops and priests—pretend nothing has happened? Doing so would, in fact, mean betraying the Gospel.

Father Amorth fought against this mentality with each blow of exorcism, but also through preaching, publishing books, giving television and radio interviews, and writing articles. He was, after all, a Paulist priest schooled in the use of multimedia as a means of evangelization. A question remains: How do we penetrate the armor of the politically correct, of the rocky certainties of weak thought that has taken over so much of our culture, media, and mores in our world, while at the same time dealing with doubts, fears, reticence, and desertions that have arisen from our own trenches?

For this reason, over the last three centuries, exorcists have practically disappeared, or at best been reduced to intolerably low numbers, from the Church. Satan has triumphed. The Church has succumbed to the devastating influence of "novelties." By wishing to adapt her eternal message to the times, she risks impoverishing it, emptying it, and betraying it. Father Amorth was not afraid to point the finger directly at the priestly formation found in modern seminaries:

> For decades in seminaries and ecclesiastical universities, a part of dogmatic theology has been removed—the part that speaks of God the Creator, of angels, of proof of their existence, and of the rebellion of demons.

Thus, in formation programs, demons no longer exist. One no longer (or almost no longer) studies spiritual theology that deals with the ordinary action of the devil, temptation, and his extraordinary action, possession and curses, and, consequently, their remedies, including exorcisms. For this reason, exorcisms are no longer believed in. This incredulity is confirmed in never having performed or witnessed one. Moral theology no longer teaches the part that deals with certain sins against the first Commandment: sorcery, necromancy, spiritism; that is, the forms of superstition most condemned by the Bible and most widespread today. For this reason, the people of God have not been catechized. And when they approach priests on these matters, they are almost always faced with a wall of ignorance and misunderstanding.[101]

Even a cursory reading of the Gospel or the writings of the saints and mystics proves to the contrary. In today's seminary and Catholic academic world, however, other texts are preferred, other stories: a very specific narrative is handed down, focusing on the most pressing themes of this world rather than the ancient Catholic faith. This narrative completely neglects, however, what Father Amorth calls "knowing the other part, that of the heavens, the dark side, the one that leads to eternal damnation." When combined with the current (modernist) mentality that wants to erase the concept of good and evil, the idea of suffering and death, what remains is a disarmed Church, unprepared for attacks by the evil one. People ask themselves how Auschwitz (that is, hell on earth) could have ever taken place.

---

[101]   Amorth, 171.

But no one seeks to understand the origin: the existence of evil that derives from the rejection of God, which is the original sin committed by Satan.

The errors of modernism are by no means limited to the seminary system. Father Amorth said that in addition to such ignorance, there are "doctrinal errors of many theologians and biblical scholars. Some even go so far as to deny exorcisms in the Gospel, considering them a 'cultural language, an adaptation to the mentality of the age.'"[102] With his typical wit, he says: "No, dear theologian, Jesus was not looking for empathy and did not possess the secret powers of a sorcerer. He possessed the omnipotence of God, and with his actions, he demonstrated that he was God. These 'subtleties' seem to escape modern theologians."[103] Elsewhere he emphasizes, "To illustrate my point, I will quote the latest statistics concerning theologians; they are particularly revealing and terrible. I say 'terrible' because they lead to the following conclusion: one out of three theologians does not believe in the existence of Satan; almost two out of three believe in his existence, but not in his practical actions, and refused to take it into account in pastoral activity. This is very little room for those who believe and try to act accordingly."[104]

This causes further damage to believers. He said, "The disbelief in the existence of Satan is widespread and does not permit people to defend themselves from the enemy, to be saved from his infernal clutches."[105]

As we have seen, however, the popes have never had any doubts in raising their voices against "the smoke of

102   Amorth, 171–72.
103   Amorth, *An Exorcist Tells*, 167.
104   Amorth, *More Stories,* 17.
105   Amorth, *L'Ultimo Esorcista*, 172.

Satan"—especially Popes Paul VI, John Paul II, and Benedict XVI. So why is the Church both unconvicted and unconvincing in warning the people of God? Father Amorth has an answer that is neither trivial nor convenient: "The bishops have a great fault in the Catholic Church."[106] It is up to them, in fact, to nominate exorcists. But few do, he says, because "they are ignorant of the matter. They haven't studied. They do not fully trust what is written in the Gospel. But above all," he says, "I am sorry to say, they have never witnessed an exorcism . . . It is difficult to believe in the existence of Satan if one has never witnessed an exorcism. I would also add that this abandonment of three centuries of the practice of exorcisms has meant that in the eyes of many, exorcisms themselves appear as something abominable, monstrous, which we should resort to absolutely as little as possible, or better, not at all."[107]

There are no exorcists in the city squares, so people resort to magicians, fortune tellers, and even satanists. Citing a 1991 government report on witchcraft in Italy, he noted that "more than twelve million Italians visit magicians, sorcerers, card readers, and so on every year."[108] Nature abhors a vacuum. This shocking statistic points to a Church hierarchy who have abdicated their specific duty written in the Gospel: to cast out demons. Father Amorth quotes the Second Vatican Council in this regard: "For a monumental struggle against the powers of darkness pervades the whole history of man. The battle was joined from the very origins of the world and will continue until the last day, as the Lord has attested." As Pope Saint John Paul II wrote, "The Church shares in Christ's victory over the devil, for Christ

---

[106]   Amorth, 172.
[107]   Amorth, 172.
[108]   Amorth, *More Stories*, 13.

has given to his disciples the power to cast out demons. The Church uses this victorious power through faith in Christ and prayer, which in particular cases can take the form of exorcism."

There is, therefore, a crisis of faith underlying the phenomenon of disbelief in the existence of Satan. Father Amorth was convinced of this. Western societies have liberated themselves from God, Catholics are a small minority, and churches and seminaries have been emptied. There is no place even for the devil: if there is no good, there is no evil; if everything is all relative, nothing is absolute. Despite the popes, the Church itself is traversed and battered by winds of crises that at times seem to be overwhelming it.

Father Amorth long pleaded of the need to return to the Gospel, to the entirety of the Gospel. He says, "'These signs will accompany those who believe: in my name they will drive out demons . . . They will lay hands on the sick, and they will recover,' says Jesus. If at least priests believed the words of the Lord and in the power they have, they would never tire of blessing all those who ask for even a simple blessing. I believe that many evils would disappear and that an army of people (magicians, fortune tellers, psychics, and the like) would end up unemployed. This is one of the goals that we exorcists have, at least indirectly."[109]

Father Amorth recalls the vision of Pope Leo XIII in 1884. He witnessed a dialogue between Jesus and Satan in which the devil claimed to be able to destroy the Church. But he needed time and asked for at least one hundred years, which Jesus granted, even if He would not have allowed the plan to be carried out. One hundred years has now arrived: it is our present era. In that vision, Leo XIII

[109]   Amorth, *L'Ultimo Esorcista*, 173.

was deeply moved and composed a prayer to the *defensor fidei*, Saint Michael the Archangel, the enemy of the devil. It was recited at the end of each Mass up until the liturgical reforms of the Second Vatican Council:

> Saint Michael the Archangel, defend us in battle. Be our protection against the wickedness and snares of the devil; May God rebuke him, we humbly pray; And do thou, O prince of the heavenly host, by the power of God, thrust into hell Satan and all evil spirits who wander through the world for the ruin of souls. Amen.

However, *non praevalebunt* (they shall not prevail). The Church belongs to God, not to man. Therefore, she can suffer, undergo trials, and fall into sin, but she shall not be overcome. Satan attacks the popes, but the popes resist. Then he attacks cardinals, bishops, priests, and religious. These are his most powerful enemies. Saint Faustina Kowalska, the Polish mystic of Divine Mercy, had a vision of hell in which she saw the place prepared by Satan for damned priests, "unworthy who had had the audacity to receive sacrilegiously in their hands and in their hearts the Son of the Virgin. Those wretches have suffered such tortures that all the ones I have talked about are nothing in comparison."

Father Amorth admitted, "It is normal that this is so. Nobody should be scandalized by this. Nor should there be any scandal if some in the Church succumb to [the devil's] flattery and allow themselves to be overcome. Priests and men and women religious are in a terrible spiritual battle. They must never give in to the devil. If they open the door of their soul to the devil, even a little, he enters and takes over their entire life."[110]

To Father Amorth, one manifestation of the work of the devil is the tragedy of pedophilia in the Church. What can be more demonic than the abuse of the little ones, the beloved of Jesus—"Let the children come to me . . . if you do not become as small as a child . . ."—the weakest and most defenseless, the essence of innocence? Father Amorth said, "It cannot be forgotten that pedophilia among the clergy has erupted in recent decades. This is the time of Satan's fury in the world. A fury that affects the Church very powerfully. The fact that the scandals have come out is good. Because it allows the Church to do penance, to repent, not to sin anymore."[111] We are at the end of the hundred years, the century, requested of Jesus by Satan in the prophetic vision of Pope Leo XIII.

It is necessary, nonetheless, that we confront reality. As long as evil exists on earth, the devil exists. From the garden of Eden to our era consisting of the most advanced and sophisticated technology, it is always he who poisons hearts and causes egoism and all the vices that derive from it. Can pedophilia—especially that in the Church—be anything other than a frightening and monstrous manifestation of egoism? The pedophile is someone who puts himself above and at the center of everything and uses others—children!—for the satanic egoism of himself and his perverse vice. It is satanic egoism elevated to the highest level. It is the victory of the devil. Father Amorth warned never to forget that

---

[110]   Amorth, 210.
[111]   Amorth, 211.

the world is in the hands of the devil's power. Satan has many prophets. There are many the Bible refers to as false prophets. They are false because they lead to lies and not to the truth. These people exist outside but also inside the Church. They can be recognized immediately. They say they speak in the name of the Church, but instead they speak in the name of the world. They ask the Church to take on the clothes of the world, and in doing so they confuse the faithful and lead the Church into waters that are not hers. They are the waters of the evil one, the waters the Bible describes in extraordinary ways in the final book, the Apocalypse.[112]

Many believe that we are living through the worst possible times. This is not the case, as every era has its share of greatness and its miseries. Other moments in history have been much more difficult and painful than the present one. It is, however, also true that between the twentieth and twenty-first centuries, evil has risen to new and unprecedented heights, aided by the great achievements of science and technology, not always placed at the service of man and his good. It is as if the devil has unleashed himself against the progress of humanity, penetrating and poisoning man from within. Father Amorth explained:

Satan's anger has existed for as long as the world has existed. But since God gave His Son, Jesus, into the world, this anger has grown stronger. Since Jesus has come, the clash between the two armies has been out in the open, head-to-head. Satan pitted the people

---

[112]   Amorth, 211.

against Christ and managed to convince them that it was necessary to kill him. The death of Jesus is the victory of Satan. But it is only an apparent victory, because in reality it is Christ who triumphs with the Resurrection. But His triumph does not erase evil. It does not erase the presence of the dragon, the beast, Satan. He is still there. But since Christ came, man can be certain that if he entrusts himself to Christ, he will be victorious. Even in the difficulty of life, he can defeat death.[113]

---

[113]   Amorth, 211–12.

12

OUR LADY ON
THE HILL

"**I**s Our Lady appearing in Yugoslavia?" was the headline of a short article that appeared in *Madre di Dio* in the November 1981 issue. Four months earlier, the world had discovered a secluded village in Yugoslavia called Medjugorje.[114] (Since 1995, it has been within the Republic of Bosnia-Herzegovina.) According to a group of six children, the Virgin Mary revealed herself there on June 24, before beginning to appear to them regularly. "From that moment," wrote Saverio Gaeta, "the attention (of Father Amorth) regarding this Marian apparition

---

[114] Father Amorth lived during the initial apparitions of Medjugorje when the Blessed Mother allegedly appeared to several children, and there were evident fruits of prayer, fasting, conversion, and a general return to the sacraments. These were undeniable evidence to Father Amorth, despite the controversy of his day. The supernatural character of the apparitions has not been confirmed or approved by the Church and remains under investigation, partly due to the ongoing nature of the alleged apparitions. Whether the ongoing visions are of supernatural origins remains to be seen and left to the prudential judgement of the Church.

never ceased. He became one of the foremost authoritative commentators on the messages revealed by the Virgin, as well as a great friend of the visionaries."

Still today, in line with mandatory prudence in similar cases, the Church has not officially or definitively made a pronouncement on Medjugorje. In the meantime, millions of pilgrims have climbed Apparition Hill and experienced unusual phenomena, in addition to conversions and healings. From the beginning, Father Amorth "was moved to openness and trust," explained Saverio Gaeta, "which subsequently became a resolute certainty" regarding the Marian apparitions. This position, in fact, would lead to numerous problems. He wrote in the article:

> As news spread, pilgrimages have increased more and more. At first, people came from nearby places, then more and more from all over Yugoslavia. Many miracles of healings and other signs have already been reported. But the most significant fact is in the religious awakening—in a land dominated by communism for forty years. The long recitation of the rosary (which is interspersed with songs and which lasts up to an hour and a half), involves Orthodox, Catholics, and Mohammedans—the three religions present in the region—united in prayer. Reception of the sacraments is very intense. By the end of September, it is estimated that there were 10,000 pilgrims a day.

He admitted in the beginning that "we know how the Church is slow to speak out on these phenomena, which first require careful study. And we, too, are cautious in reporting facts of this nature in our newspaper, which we want to examine first." But later he would be convinced of the authenticity of the apparitions. Our Lady chose precisely that inaccessible place in the heart of the evil Communist empire. (The apparitions began eight years before the fall of the Berlin wall.)

The bishop of Mostar, the diocese that encompasses Medjugorje, Monsignor Pavao Žanić, with due prudence, initially said he was convinced of the good faith of the visionaries (He later changed his mind). Above all, ever more numerous crowds flocked to the hill, while the Church eventually opened the Medjugorje dossier. Apparitions took place one after the other, according to the six young people, in which the Virgin Mary invited listeners to prayer, conversion, penance, fasting, and peace. Long lines of penitents began to form for confession to the point that more confessors were needed; the Franciscan friars who administered the parish of Saint James were too few. Unexplained phenomena of an apparent miraculous nature increased.

Father Amorth was present at an apparition his first time in April 1984. It took place at the parish of Saint James in the presence of four of the six visionaries, Ivanka, Jakov, Marija, and Vicka. He wrote about it in *Madre di Dio*:

> Standing at the wall altar, above which is a crucifix, they make the sign of the cross and begin to pray together aloud. After a while, they fall to their knees in perfect unison. From that moment on, they are completely oblivious to what is happening around them. Their eyes are open but not fixed on anything. They do not react to anything; they are not disturbed by the strong flashes of the cameras close to their faces, by noises, nor by a doctor who examines them. They all just contemplate the vision. At a certain point, in

unison, remaining on their knees, they recite the Our Father and the Glory be. Our Lady said the first part (Our Father . . .), while they continue, "who art in heaven." Then the dialogue with Vicka resumes. After a few moments pass, the young people raise their arms as if wanting to follow the vision: She goes away! They stand up, and we hurry to church for Mass.

He followed his narration of events with some personal considerations:

What impressed us most was the prayer and composure of the people. We went during a "slow" period, as we wanted to avoid the crowds during the holiday and summer period. In addition to us, there was only a small group of Germans. But the church was full from 5:00 p.m. to 7:30 p.m. One observes that the words of Our Lady have been taken seriously. Even the bishop of Mostar admitted to us with all certainty that prayer and fasting are intense and there are many conversions. He also admitted that there has been a radical change in the people in the area. Other things have been confirmed to us by Father Tomislav. For example, monthly confession is attended meticulously; it takes place three days a month: Thursday, Friday, and Saturday before the first Sunday of each month. It is also an occasion for peace among the neighbors. The rivalries that were once strong between families no longer exist. Instead, there is peace.

Undoubtedly, something happened in Medjugorje and continues to take place. Even the most skeptical have been forced to admit as much. Sooner or later, the Church will make its pronouncement. In the meantime, articles, books, and media interviews continue to report on the numerous powerful experiences of pilgrims. Scientists debate it, bishops and cardinals visit the village and question the visionaries, and the fame of the Bosnian village spreads throughout the world.

Father Amorth continued speaking about Medjugorje:

> If you ask us for an opinion, in a personal capacity, we repeat the saying of the Gospel: "A tree is known by its fruits." We didn't go to see extraordinary things (and we didn't see any), but we went to see if the fruits were good. We definitively answer yes. There are good fruits, because they are based on the Gospel. If it turns out that there are not enough elements to confirm that Our Lady has appeared to the young people, the messages that the young people have attributed to Our Lady would always remain true. That is, every bishop and priest would continue to strongly recommend prayer, fasting, conversion, faith in God, and the last things. I can understand that it is difficult [to believe in] a succession of apparitions that have been continuing daily for almost three years and that show no signs of abating. In response to such objections, Our Lady allegedly said that they are the final ones for humanity during this epoch. There may be other reasons for confusion, because it is never simple to verify supernatural events. To us, however, it is legitimate to make a personal judgment. For example, there was a woman who went to Medjugorje and found herself suddenly cured of cancer. She went to a priest and asked him: "Excuse me, Father, if I had waited for the judgment of the hierarchy, do you think I would be healed?"

Father Amorth was the editor-in-chief of a Marian magazine, the famous Mariologist who "clung" to the mantle of the Virgin. For this reason, he could not ignore Medjugorje. He delved deep into the phenomenon and devoted much space and attention to it. From December 1984 until 1988, he published a column he called "The Medjugorje Corner" in *Madre di Dio*. It was well read and received many comments.

In the first column, he listed "the detectable effects" of the events that had occurred in those three years: "1. As of this writing, tens of thousands of Italians have gone on pilgrimage to Medjugorje. 2. More and more books, booklets, and pamphlets have been published with a wide circulation, demonstrating how much the topic is being received. 3. Many existing prayer groups, and newly formed ones, have been stimulated by those events to meet for longer periods, with increased participation, and are more efficacious. 4. Various centers have also sprung up, all throughout Italy, both to organize pilgrimages to Medjugorje and to prolong the efficacy [after return]."

In a long and detailed letter, he explained his position to the bishop of Mostar, stating, among other things:

> I have studied these things in depth, albeit limited to the point of view that was possible to me and in accordance with my abilities. I have studied the messages attributed to the Blessed Virgin, and I have studied the effects of these messages on the people. I find the messages excellent: they are conformed to the Gospel and practical in exemplary implementation. Above all, I have noticed their great efficaciousness on the people. I have witnessed conversions, intensification of prayer that is lasting, a renewal of

fasting (now relegated by ecclesiastical laws to the good will of individuals), and people returning to the faith. These are realities that I have touched and done so with my own hand. When I see that those who go to Medjugorje often have (of course, not always) an effect that leads to a continually greater commitment to Christian life, I cannot say, "Do not go there"; but, rather, I say: "Go there."

Moreover, was Saint Padre Pio not "looked down upon" within the Church itself by priests, bishops, and cardinals who advised against going on pilgrimage to San Giovanni Rotondo? In this regard, Father Amorth quoted a friend of his, a lawyer from Modena, who bantered, "I do not understand you priests. People do not pray, they do not go to church, they do not receive the sacraments. But here is [Padre Pio] who attracts crowds: he takes them to church, takes them to pray, takes them to the sacraments. And this seems to make you [clergy] angry. Instead of encouraging this, you do everything to dissuade it."

Father Amorth could not accept or tolerate that the faithful were discouraged or even forbidden from going on pilgrimage to Bosnia. He saw the fruits of conversion, and the defeat of Satan, in the long confession lines. As he wrote in his groundbreaking book on exorcism, "Many times I have written that Satan is much more enraged when we take souls away from him through confession than when we take away bodies through exorcism."[115] Thus, he eventually took a stand against a letter from the Congregation for the Doctrine of the Faith that asked the Italian bishops to "publicly discourage" trips to Medjugorje, "as well as any

---

[115] Amorth, *An Exorcist Tells*, 67.

other form of promotion, especially publications," which could distract or disrupt the work of the Vatican commission charged with shedding light on those facts. He replied as follows:

> We are faced with a very serious fact, which calls into question the role of the most delicate and important dicastery of the Church and, in our opinion, the very concept of the Church, as Vatican II has endeavored to highlight. The first question we ask ourselves is why that dicastery, which intervenes only when a question of faith or morals is under discussion, is involved in a simple disciplinary question, debatable, addressing the Italian Episcopate as if it only concerned Italy, creating a dangerous precedent on the functions and limits of the dicastery itself. The intervention is aimed less at *promotion*, which is one of the current aims of that dicastery, but instead at suffocating and repressing. All this to reach the final sentence: to urge the Italian bishops to "discourage pilgrimages." Why? Do they do harm? Are the pilgrims—over five million so far who have gone there to pray, to receive the sacraments, to make resolutions to live a better life—to be condemned? Have there been any disorder or negative aspects? These are questions that Monsignor Bovone [secretary of the CDF, signatory of the letter] does not even ask. He speaks generically of confusion among the faithful and obstacles to the work of the commission, but he does not cite examples of either one. And he seems to ignore that, in these cases, popular piety has always preceded ecclesiastical decisions and is itself the object of examination. It also remains to be seen whether and to what

extent it is legitimate to prohibit going to a place to pray without unduly infringing on the freedom of the children of God. There are no places where it is forbidden to pray! So are unwarranted prohibitions binding regarding obedience? Or do they not instead damage the credibility of the authorities that issue them? It seems then completely anachronistic, especially in our era, to deal with this in the press. It is ridiculous to try to suppress information, especially regarding something of worldwide relevance. On the other hand, it should have been recognized that many writings about Medjugorje—the result of careful and prolonged studies done on site—are a valuable aid for investigating. Here another discourse should be inserted: the discourse of the Church. Ecclesiastical authority acts within the bosom of the Church, but it alone is not the Church. It has the task of discerning, which no one denies; but first it must know how to listen. It must look with gratitude on the one who, intelligently and competently, painstakingly provides the results of serious studies, rather than appearing irritated by that person, as if he were unduly engaged in things that did not concern him.[116]

In short, for Father Amorth, the Medjugorje dossier could not be liquidated by authority. He dedicated significant space to it in his Marian magazine to the point that he was soon met with severe resistance, misunderstandings, and opposition—even in the Pauline world. Serious criticisms also arrived from ecclesial circles to the point that he

---

[116] Gaeta, *L'eredità segreta di don Amorth*, 201–3.

was forced to respond in *Madre di Dio* in December 1985. With his typical passion, he wrote:

> Can it be said that our newspaper has dealt with this issue too much? We reply that, inasmuch as we are a Marian newspaper, such an event warrants a level of interest that certainly exceeds what may be applicable in other publications. And the seriousness of our investigations leads us to declare that we have nothing to rectify regarding what we have previously written in such abundance. The messages have continued—with such evangelical content—on prayer, fasting, conversion, and frequenting the sacraments. The fact that the messages have been received is confirmed by the torrent of over five million pilgrims who have been to Medjugorje from all parts of the world. We have individually questioned hundreds of them and we have not yet met a single one who has returned disappointed or sorry. The number of conversions, of those returning to sincere prayer and to a vitalizing Christianity, is incalculable.

If so many people have discovered spiritual consolation on the hill of Bosnia-Herzegovina and have returned to God and to the Church, why interfere? If the evangelical tree is justified by its fruits and the fruits are good, did Jesus not say "who is not against us, is with us"? Father Amorth merely gave an account—as a Mariologist, as a journalist, and as a Pauline—of what had taken place in Medjugorje and after Medjugorje. The wind of the Spirit blows where it wills, and no one can—or should—stop it.

As such, he explained in 1986, "For over four years I have been studying the facts and have collected

documentation. I have published only what I have personally ascertained (I have collaborated on three volumes and
I have written about sixty articles) and have found useful
for the good of souls. For this reason, I have not published
many other studies . . . I do not think they would do good."
Among the things he did not publish were topics regarding the internal disputes within the Diocese of Mostar,
tensions between the Franciscans and the diocesan clergy,
friars suspended *a divinis* (a canonical removal of clerical
rights), and controversy over the bishop's position. These
were secondary issues, which risked polluting the judgment on everything else.

At the end of that year, having already begun his service
as an exorcist a few months earlier, Father Amorth took a
stand: "After having studied these issues from all possible
points of view, I affirm: In my opinion, it is impossible that
Our Lady is not appearing in Medjugorje. Although I have
never seen her in five years, I have very clearly seen signs of
her presence, the effects of her presence, and transforma-
tions brought about by her presence."[117]

Saverio Gaeta wrote, "Don Amorth constantly went
deeper into the messages of the Queen of Peace given to the
visionary Marija Pavloviÿ beginning in 1984, in particular
in his column in *Madre di Dio* and in the meetings he held
every last Saturday of the month in a Roman parish." From
1985 onwards, he presented to his readers and listeners the
fruits of his personal research and studies on Medjugorje
in a text that noted how "the many aspects touched upon
(in the apparitions) are all contained in revelation, even if
particular accentuations are evident." That is, there is nothing in the words of the Virgin revealed to the visionaries

---

[117]   Gaeta, 210–11.

that contrast with the truths of the faith proclaimed by the Church over twenty centuries.

He summarized, as a priest, exorcist, and Mariologist, the content and meaning of the messages:

1. God exists; in God there is life; whoever finds God, finds life. The existence of God is the fundamental presupposition of religion, and we do not believe that there has been such insistence on this in other apparitions. Instead, it has become urgent for our society, characterized by atheism taught to the masses. This is a characteristic of Medjugorje, as it is the insistence in the Creed, the sum of the truths of our faith. 2. The constant call for peace. Our Lady introduced herself saying, "I am the Queen of Peace." All the other messages also seem to focus on this theme of peace: a return to God, sincere conversion, prayer, fasting. . . . Many consider the theme of peace as the main topic of these apparitions. 3. Prayer, fasting, sacraments. These are constant calls in the latest apparitions approved by the Church: La Salette, Lourdes, Fatima. Here we notice something new: exemplification, going into details. For prayer: it is recommended at a minimum the daily recitation of seven Our Fathers, Hail Marys, Glory Bes, and the Creed; but it is also recommended to pray for half an hour in the morning and half an hour in the evening, while more prolonged prayer is recommended for the most generous. Fasting: it is recommended on bread and water; for those more generous, beyond only Fridays. . . . Mass and sacraments: daily Mass attendance is encouraged; for confessions, it is said: if Christians were to confess once a month, entire regions would soon be healed

spiritually. 4. Other Gospel truths repeated: the last things, God's judgment, the existence of Satan. Among the precepts of Christ, the insistence on charity predominates, in particular on the most difficult and heroic aspect of it, love of one's enemies. In this, one cannot fail to see an invitation to human fraternity; the Virgin presents herself as the Mother of all humanity, as God is the Father of all. And one cannot fail to see in this teaching a confirmation of the ecumenical spirit of Vatican II, especially if one considers that these invitations are addressed in Yugoslavia where Catholics, Orthodox, Muslims, and atheists coexist. The conformity of these teachings with the Gospel and with the praxis of the Church is immediately evident. No new devotions are suggested; there is no practice that introduces novelties.[118]

He also commented positively on the credibility of the visionaries:

They have been continuously examined by various medical teams from different countries (Italian, French, Austrian, Yugoslav) and with the use of the most sophisticated means, as only modern science can offer; examinations of this type were never possible in the past. The results have already been published in four volumes, which everyone can check in any bookstore. There is no doubt about the soundness of the visionaries: to the exclusion of any pathologies, to the exclusion of any fraud or coercion, or to the fact that the phenomenon of their ecstasies is not

---

[118]   Gaeta, 217–18.

humanly explicable. To these observations we add: the spiritual journey that these young people have made and are making is a wonderful and verifiable path by anyone who knows them even a little. Consider the heroic charity they demonstrate in making themselves available to visitors, in taking on grueling fatigue, and exercising limitless patience. It is a miracle they have not been committed to an asylum . . . And let us add: all six have experienced physical and moral sufferings, interior and outward. We are not canonizing anyone. We are only giving testimony of what can be verified by anyone. Only the Lord measures holiness.[119]

As previously noted, Father Amorth stepped down as editor-in-chief of *Madre di Dio* in 1988 to devote himself exclusively to the ministry of exorcisms. It is not a stretch to suggest that the controversies of Medjugorje—at least partially—played a part in his departure. In the final editorial, December, Father Amorth returned to the question of the Marian apparitions:

In recent years, they have increased throughout the world at an increasing rate that cannot leave us indifferent. And so, as René Laurentin observed, Christians sensitive to these phenomena find themselves caught between two camps: "Prudence!" say the priests; "When an apparition is not recognized, do not go there, do not talk about it." On the other hand, the message says: "Urgency!" And if it is truly Our Lady who is appearing and calling us, not taking

[119]   Gaeta, 218–19.

notice would imply culpability. How can we settle the dichotomy? Laurentin himself points out how prudence and urgency can be connected. Inasmuch as the Marian messages recall the Gospel in their essential content (return to God, conversion, penance, prayer, fasting), then they have the same urgency as the Gospel which they echo. In this, they are an alarm bell in today's society that has quietly and happily surrendered to sin. Prudence, however, is required for study in order to declare whether an apparition is authentic or not. Even if, in the meantime, the golden rule always remains that of the Gospel: "A tree is known by its fruits." . . . Regarding the facts and events, I have always sought to report the truth after careful research—even if I stepped on the toes of some in doing so. I do not claim [my viewpoint] has always been shared by everyone. But I am grateful to those who understood and appreciated this effort.

Medjugorje remains an open question to this day. Father Gabriele Amorth made his contribution in study, research, and development—certainly aware of the urgency in witnessing to the presence of the Virgin on the Bosnian hill, alongside the prudence of knowing that God's time (and that of His Church) is not the same as man's. One day we will know. In the meantime, he offered his personal testimony with his signature passion, honesty, and sincerity. And he accepted the price he was forced to pay.

13

KILLED BY THE DEVIL

By now, Father Amorth had become a TV and radio star. He spoke about the devil (and more) on Radio Maria to a large listenership, published numerous books that sold well, and was called on as an expert to appear on various television programs to talk about possible "satanic" events. Those were years of intense popularity. He was by far the most well-known and famous exorcist. He was sought after by the suffering, listened to, and adored by countless admirers.

There were also those who were annoyed by him. He was the priest who was always speaking about the devil on television shows or promoting the authenticity of the Medjugorje apparitions. None of the criticism mattered to him. Father Gabriele Amorth had too much to do to be bothered by trivial issues. As long as his health permitted, he continued doing exorcisms. He promoted, whenever possible, the cause of exorcism among bishops and priests and warned believers and unbelievers alike about the presence of the devil.

At this time, the Church began to revise the Rite of Exorcism and liturgical texts dealing with exorcism, in line with the updating that followed the Second Vatican Council. Once again, he had to take on what he referred to as "the incredulity of the Vatican regarding the existence of Satan." Father Amorth and other exorcists thought they would be consulted by the special commission of cardinals regarding the matter. Instead, the new Rite of Exorcism was written by a team of liturgists with absolutely no experience in the field of exorcism. "Nothing," he wrote, regarding the hierarchy's inclusion of the experience of exorcists in the new ritual. Then, "Surprisingly, on 4 June, 1990 a new ritual appeared *ad interim*, without any of us having been consulted, not even verbally or by telephone."

The text was sent to exorcists so they could experiment with it in the field, then send feedback to the bishops, the episcopal conferences, and the Congregation of Divine Worship. Incredibly, what eventually happened—also due to the fact that there were too many participants involved—was that "nothing arrived at the Vatican. Nothing," said Father Amorth. He continued, "We exorcists had much to say. The revision and proof of the new ritual was, in actuality, a total disaster for us. It was all too evident that the new ritual had been prepared by people who had never performed or witnessed an exorcism in their lives."[120]

As such, eighteen exorcists of different nationalities met, discussed, and wrote down their observations, which they delivered "to the Italian Episcopal Conference and the Congregation for Divine Worship and gave a copy directly to Pope John Paul II who took it and thanked them." On November 22, 1998 the official version of the new ritual was

---

[120]   Amorth, *L'Ultimo Esorcista*, 178.

promulgated. Father Amorth recalled that "our disappointment was immense. To our dismay, the final text was basically the same as the *ad interim* edition, with the addition of some enormous errors." He cited a few:

> The text prohibited the use of exorcism in cases of curses, which are responsible for over ninety percent of diabolical disturbances. Further, the text forbade exorcisms without the certainty of the presence of the devil. This is absurd. Only by doing an exorcism can one be sure that there is possession or not! In addition, those who wrote this text did not realize they were contradicting the *Catechism of the Catholic Church*, which states that exorcisms should be done both in cases of possession, as well as disturbances caused by the devil. In these types of disturbances, there is never possession; that is, there is never the presence of the devil inside the body of people—just as he is not present when animals, houses, and objects are exorcised.[121]

None of the observations of the eighteen exorcists were received or given consideration. "They were only useful in being scorned," commented Father Amorth. Within the Congregation for Divine Worship, [the eighteen] were accused of promoting "a campaign against the rite," and Father Amorth himself of even having made an "indecent accusation."[122] Their voices, however, were eventually heard. Fortunately, Father Amorth recalls, "*In extremis*, Cardinal Jorge Arturo Medina Estevez, who became prefect of the

---

121   Amorth, 179.
122   Amorth, 179.

Congregation for Divine Worship in 1996, managed at the last minute to insert a particular notification, in which he personally allowed exorcists to use the old ritual by making a request to the bishop. This was our salvation. We were all able to continue to exorcise with the old ritual, which, in my opinion, is the only effective one against the devil."[123]

It must be said that Cardinal Joseph Ratzinger—who at the time was prefect of the Doctrine of the Faith and a member of the commission for the revision of the rite of exorcism—had an important role (in a positive sense) in the saga. "He was the only one to seek out and listen to the opinion of us exorcists, even if, unfortunately, this opinion was not shared by his collaborators," commented Father Amorth. The future Pope Benedict XVI understood that the experience of front-line priests was important, and he went out in search of it. Father Amorth worked as an exorcist under two Pontiffs who believed in the presence of Satan. As we have documented, Popes John Paul II and Benedict XVI were powerful, recognized enemies of the devil, who both feared and attacked them.

Both popes spoke openly and often about Satan. Regarding Karol Wojtyla, Father Amorth recalled, "it is known that he performed several exorcisms in Vatican."[124] He mentioned two. The first took place on March 27, 1982 when the archbishop of Spoleto, Monsignor Ottorino Alberti, accompanied a girl named Francesca to him. Upon seeing him, she began to scream and throw herself on the ground. The pope ordered the devil to get out of her several times to no avail. "She suddenly calmed down only when John Paul II told her he would say a Mass for her the next

---

[123]   Amorth, 180.
[124]   Amorth, 184.

day."[125] The pope himself was disturbed and confessed to Monsignor Jacques Martin, prefect of the papal household, that he had "never seen such a thing, something of biblical proportions." Francesca returned to the pope, free, years later. She had gotten married and had two children.

The second exorcism dealt with another girl, Sabrina, who was suffering from a very difficult case of diabolical possession. Every Wednesday, she went to Father Amorth to be exorcised. Once, he decided to take her to the papal audience in Saint Peter's Square. Father Amorth described what happened:

> When John Paul II arrives in the square, she starts screaming. It takes ten people to hold her. She wants to throw herself at the pope. Her face is full of hatred. She drools. There is blasphemy. Her body quivers. She is like a beast ready to attack. The audience ends and those who have accompanied Sabrina are exhausted. During the audience, the pope notices this woman. He hears her screams. He inquires and tells his secretary, Fr. Stanislaw Dziwisz, to bring her to him. The papal car returns from the arch by the bells and stops just ahead, next to the basilica, in an area out of sight and inaccessible to the faithful. Sabrina is brought there. She is in a trance. Her eyes are two white sockets. She drools with her head tilted back. As soon as she is brought close to the pope, she begins to scream and tremble. "No, no, leave me alone. Leave me alone!" she shouts. The pope exorcises her on the spot. He blesses her several times and then lets her be.[126]

---

[125]   Amorth, 184.
[126]   Amorth, 185.

That was only the first salvo, and the enemy was pre-pared to counterattack. In the afternoon session with Father Amorth found Sabrina still possessed. He said that she had, "in fact, a profound case of possession, one deeply rooted."[127] During the exorcism, "the devil is infuriated by the encounter with the pope, but at the same time, he feels strengthened because the exorcism of John Paul II was not able to defeat him. He feels strong and wants to show me he is strong."[128] Then, before Father Amorth's eyes, something extraordinary took place: the devil made the possessed girl walk on the wall. Afterwards, she was unable to recall anything. She would be freed years later, but, said Father Amorth, "I am convinced that, in some way, the exorcism performed by Wojtyla left its mark on her."[129]

Pope Benedict XVI, a lifelong academic and theolo-gian, probably never performed any exorcisms. The theme of the devil, nonetheless, was present in his sermons. Once, in 2009, he came into contact with two possessed people under the care of Father Amorth. They were accompanied by two women to the audience in Saint Peter's Square in the hopes of some benefit. As Father Amorth explains, "It is not a mystery that many of the pope's gestures and words infuriate Satan. It is no mystery that even the presence of the pope alone disturbs and in some way helps the pos-sessed in their battle against the one who possesses them." Upon the arrival of Benedict XVI, the two began to fidget and shake, their teeth chattering. As the popemobile made its way through the square, they threw themselves on the ground, hit their heads on the stones, and uttered fright-ening howls.

---

[127]   Amorth, 185.
[128]   Amorth, 186.
[129]   Amorth, 186.

At that point, according to Father Amorth:

Benedict XVI turns around, but does not come near. He sees the two women and the two young men on the ground screaming, drooling, trembling, and enraged. He sees the hateful gaze of the two men directed at him. The pope is not upset. He looks on from afar. He raises his arm and blesses the four. For the two possessed, it is a furious shock, like a whip cracked over their bodies. It is so strong they are knocked to the ground and fall three meters back. Now they are no longer screaming. Instead, they cry, cry, and cry. They moan throughout the entire audience. When the pope leaves, they come back to themselves and cannot remember a thing.[130]

Father Amorth commented:

Benedict XVI is greatly feared by Satan. His masses, blessings, and words are like powerful exorcisms. I do not believe that Benedict XVI performs exorcisms, or at least I'm not aware if he does. However, I believe that his entire pontificate is a great exorcism against Satan. Effective and powerful. It is a great exorcism that should be of much benefit to those bishops and cardinals who do not believe: they will have to answer for their unbelief. Not believing and, above all, not appointing exorcists where there is an explicit need is, in my opinion, a grave sin, a mortal sin.[131]

---

[130] Amorth, 183.
[131] Amorth, 183–84.

The greatness of the two popes (and the sainthood of one of them) unfortunately did not prevent scandals. Linked to the two powerful themes of money and sex, scandal rocked the Vatican at the turn of the century. In the shadow of the sacred palaces, among so many honest and pure souls, characters with questionable morals were also roaming, and worse preying. Sordid affairs, one after another, have come to light. The popes tried to intervene, but were unsuccessful in removing the "filth" from the darkest recesses of the Vatican.

And not just the Vatican. Amplified by a bloodthirsty media, horrendous stories about unworthy clergy have circulated around the globe involving religious, bishops, priests, and also lay people. It's been a litany of painful and dramatic stories of wounded people, often irreparably, and the wounding of the reputation of the Catholic Church itself. Books have been published, investigations reported on, and the phenomenon of corruption seems unstoppable. Pope Francis strived to put a stop to it, with mixed results. The Barque of Peter is caught in the storm. And then Covid-19 arrived to further complicate an already difficult situation.

According to Father Amorth, there is someone behind all this—a single agent. His name is Satan:

> He attacks priests and those consecrated to God, above all, because by striking a priest, he can drag many others to hell. We think of all those priests who have soiled their garments through the sexual abuse of minors. These are demonic acts. What can be more perverse than such a thing? Satan is total perversion. It is he who enters hearts and leads people to actions like this. The devil attacks priests more than anyone. There is only one way not to be overcome: by prayer

and fasting. A priest who sexually abuses a child causes an avalanche of suffering and destruction. It is a most grievous fault. This is the greatest victory of Satan over the Church: convincing those people who should be exclusively of Christ to work for the opposite—exclusively for the devil.[132]

Jesus's terrible words come to mind: "Whoever causes one of these little ones who believe in me to sin, it would be better for him to have a great millstone hung around his neck and to be drowned in the depths of the sea" (cf. Mt 18:6). As long as he was physically able, therefore, Father Amorth never tired of warning of the power of Satan, his menacing presence, and his ability to conquer the hearts, minds, and bodies of so many good and simple people.

In reality, however, Father Amorth clearly states that the "majority of those who call an exorcist do not need exorcism, but a real conversion.[133] A Paulist at heart, he often used the most ordinary means of modern media to get that message out. Yet, he knew that the enemy also used modern media for his own "messaging" of lies and distortions. Take the internet, for example. In and of itself, it is an instrument for good. And yet, it can be a possible vehicle of the devil. As Father Amorth explained:

Once, I happened to search the word "Satan" on the internet. I soon had at my fingertips instructions on how to follow Satan, how to enter a satanic sect, and, effectively, how to lose one's life into nothingness . . . The internet has made information on Satanism

---

[132]   Amorth, 192.
[133]   Amorth, *More Stories,* 11.

more accessible than in the past. With a simple click, one can find satanic sects and contact them. The risk is particularly high for young people who are emotionally fragile or find themselves in difficult circumstances. If a teenager experiencing hardship goes on the internet to seek solutions and help to his or her problems, he or she can easily come in contact with these sects. It can be the beginning of the end for them. The internet is full of people who, even out of simple curiosity, come across videos that would be better never to see. They are viewed, and Satan acts. It doesn't take much. Even through a simple film, Satan can plant a bad seed in someone's heart . . . One cannot generalize, but it really can be the beginning of the end—the beginning of a spiral that leads farther and farther down. Satan enters people's lives discreetly, almost intangibly. But then, little by little, he gains ground until he has completely taken over the soul. The more ground he gains, the more difficult it is to escape. The internet is not absolute evil, but on the web, unfortunately, absolute evil is present. There he acts. And there are those who let themselves be lured.[134]

The devil uses modern means of communication, which are powerful, useful, and captivating. Awareness and vigilance must be increased. Why? What is it about the internet? Father Amorth responded by saying that it is "in large part, a world without God. And who is king in a world without God? Satan. It is no coincidence that Satan has free reign especially where there is no God. This holds

---

[134]   Amorth, *L'Ultimo Esorcista*, 156–57.

true in part in the internet world, and in part in the real
world. Where there is no God, the devil reigns. He reigns
and possesses people."[135]

Another instrument of Satan to be on guard against,
according to Father Amorth, is so-called satanic rock. As
he explains:

> I don't want [my words] to be exploited. I definitely
> do not want to say that all rock is perverse and leads
> to Satan. This is not so, and I absolutely deny it. But
> there is satanic rock, and it is this type of music I'm
> thinking of when I speak of other forms of spreading
> Satanism beyond the sects. What does satanic rock
> do? It preaches the most absolute form of nihilism.
> It battles the Catholic religion and any and all social
> order. It teaches that everything is licit, and the indi-
> vidual is God. It leads to hatred of the Church. Satanic
> rock has an open enemy: Christ and the Church, and
> only one goal—that of leading humanity to dedica-
> tion to Satan and, therefore, to self-destruction. Due
> to this type of music and the friendships formed
> among those who listen to it, many young people
> often fall into darkness, the occult.[136]

He cites as an example Marilyn Manson, the famous
American singer, who is "completely a slave to the devil,"
according to Father Amorth. He warned the parents of
young people who listen to satanic rock:

---

[135]   Amorth, 157.
[136]   Amorth, 152–53.

When I say these things, some people laugh. In the press, I am often made fun of for these statements of mine. I would like to say to those who laugh: go talk to the parents of young people who are no longer here today because they fell into the spiral of Satanism. Go laugh in their faces if you dare. I say it again. I would like to say to parents who have children who listen to satanic music: save them by accompanying them from their early teenage years. Educate them in the faith. Bring them to church even as babies. Even if they cry and run all over the church, bring them anyway. Through osmosis, they are educated in the faith.[137]

Too many rock singers are inspired by Satan. They're playing with fire. Looking for powerful emotions, too many young people fall into it. It is a spiral from which they risk never escaping, and it can have tragic and irreparable consequences. Many of these artists are linked to satanic sects, especially in the United States, where the Church of Satan originated and in which Marilyn Manson is a priest. They transmit devastating messages.

In Father Amorth's experience, "it is a form of brainwashing that leads nowhere but to abomination, homicidal fury, and self-destruction. The negative messages put forth in this music are dangerous seeds cast into the souls of young people. They have pure souls that are easily contaminated. In recent years, satanic rock has become fashionable and is now expressed in the most extreme forms. Record

---

[137]   Amorth, 153.

covers are full of blasphemous images, the lyrics incite hatred and violence towards Christians."[138]

In short, the devil uses modern media to weaken souls and bodies. Among these, music is certainly among the most powerful, as it has a broad reach, without checks or censorship. Father Amorth further explains that the devil also uses apparently innocent tools, which he transforms and broadcasts in poisonous messages, especially for small children. There are certain comics, for example, "that praise Satan." Then there is the television itself, which is present in practically every household on the planet. "The images don't always help. Indeed, children often thrive on the idea that one finds happiness in life only through money, sex, and power. Money, sex, power: the three idols dearest to Satan."

In addition, he notes how sorcerers and gurus often use television and its power for their scams. They thrive on the poverty of spirit of so many simple souls. We must stay away from these people. Father Amorth said over and over:

> In addition to good seers, there are bad ones. How do we recognize them? Simple. They ask for money. Money is the first temptation of the devil. Because with money one can buy anything: sex, drugs, plea-sure, and power. Most psychics today are false, and you should run from them. They make deals with the devil, and they are constantly asking for money. Always money. They are never satisfied. "Come back in a week and bring more money," they say. They have people queuing up outside their house. They want publicity. They are the opposite of true seers who hide

---

[138]   Amorth, 155.

their charism. These people allow God to bring people to them, and they do not want money. They know that money can lead to hell, and they flee from it.[139]

There was a well-known case regarding Sathya Sai Baba, an Indian "healer" who drew immense crowds. He was a false prophet who profited from people's innocence for a long time. He died in 2011. Father Amorth once worked with one of his victims. He spoke about it:

> I understood while exorcising [this victim] that Sai Baba was a false holy man with close ties to Satan. To me, he is Satan's beloved son on earth—a beloved son like few others in the world. He creates magic and false miracles that lead to nihilism. He makes thousands of people his followers. He leads these people to perdition and then abandons them, lost in their despair. They take the bait, because not everyone is able to make objects appear out of thin air. Not everyone is able to walk a few centimeters off the ground or do amazing, apparently inexplicable things. These things are not for everyone, but those who become children of Satan know how to do such things.[140]

Sai Baba's followers considered him a god, obeyed him, and filled his pockets with money: "Everyone hoped to be healed by him, but no one was really healed. Sai Baba was the firstborn son of Satan. I have no doubts about this. He spoke well of everyone, of Jesus in particular, but his god was one: he and he alone. He thought this of himself. He helped

---

139   Amorth, 141.
140   Amorth, 151.

hospitals in Indian villages through conspicuous donations, apparently doing good because the devil is very clever. Many Italian tourists, especially women, fell into his trap."[141]

As the world becomes increasingly interconnected through social media, Satan's presence and power are more keenly seen and felt. The thirty-year ministry of Fr. Gabriele Amorth against him were not limited to exorcism. His mission also included prevention, education, and formation—all which could not exclude faith. That is, to fight the devil and prevent him from stealing souls and bodies from God, it is first of all necessary to believe in his existence. Indeed, war cannot be waged against something or someone who does not exist. Once again, Father Amorth challenges us to turn to the Gospel, in which the actions of the enemy against Jesus are evident and concrete. From there, we must build a dam against the attacks of the evil one. Otherwise, we are building our foundation on the sand, effectively yielding and delivering ourselves over to him and his power.

His apostolate revealed how faith and the tools of prayer, penance, and fasting are the weapons feared by Satan. Against them, he can do nothing. If one has faith, he can move mountains. With faith, then, can the enemy of God not be conquered? Therefore, every day it is necessary to repel the attacks of the devil and at the same time strengthen the defenses of the people against him. He is always on the prowl, poised for the most terrible and sudden actions to drag his victims into the dark canyon of evil and carry out his heinous, demonic works.

Father Amorth recalled an awful event that shocked all of Italy, though it had a surprising ending. God's victory,

---

[141] Amorth, 152.

in fact, was revealed where it seemed Satan had won. On Sunday, June 6, 2021 the Catholic Church declared Sister Maria Laura Mainetti as Blessed. On a windy day, the people's faces masked as an anti-Covid-19 measure, the beatification took place at the sports stadium in Chiavenna (province of Sondrio) in the Diocese of Como. Presiding over the ceremony was Cardinal Marcello Semeraro, prefect of the Congregation for the Causes of Saints, with the approval of Pope Francis. Sister Mainetti belonged to the Congregation of the Daughters of the Cross, and was killed "*in odium fidei*" (in hatred of the faith) on June 6, 2000—exactly twenty-one years earlier—by three underaged girls who lured her into their trap.

The three—Ambra Gianasso, Veronica Pietrobelli, and Milena De Giambattista—were bored and numbed through listening to satanic rock music. They plotted to offer a victim to Satan. Who knows how they came to that decision, of the darkness that had overtaken their souls. They wanted to kill the parish priest, but he was saved by his robust physique. So they chose a sister, someone who was generous with everyone and would certainly come to anyone's aid. They plotted that Ambra, seventeen years of age, would call her, lying that she had been raped and was now pregnant. "Come," she said. Sister Maria Laura took the bait. How could she not respond to such a request? It was almost 10:00 p.m. when she left the convent and went unknowingly to her death.

Ambra was waiting for her with two friends. They lured her to a deserted, isolated park where drug addicts and prostitutes loitered. First, they threw rocks at her, then they finished her off by stabbing her nineteen times. On her knees, she tried to dissuade them. Then, with her last strength, she asked God to forgive them. She died at their hands, as an offering to Satan, who had invaded the minds and hearts of three bored girls. But the holy sister offered herself to God with the words of Christ: "Forgive them, for they know not what they do." The girls were arrested, convicted, and paid their debt to society. Eventually, they were released with new identities.

Today, the sister is known as Blessed Maria Laura Mainetti. A stone stained with her blood was placed at the altar during her beatification. She will be remembered by the Church on June 6. There was no need for a miracle, because she died a martyr as a witness of the faith, in hatred of God, during a vile satanic rite. In the case of martyrdom, nothing else is needed for someone to be determined Blessed.

In Rome, on the solemnity of Corpus Domini, 2021, Pope Francis recalled the event during the Angelus: "Today in Chiavenna, in the Diocese of Como, Sister Maria Laura Mainetti of the Daughters of the Cross was beatified. She was killed twenty-one years ago by three girls under the influence of a satanic sect. Such cruelty! She, who loved young people more than anything, loved and forgave those same girls who were imprisoned by evil. Sister Maria Laura left us her life project: 'Do every little thing with faith, love, and enthusiasm.' May the Lord give all of us faith, love, and enthusiasm. A round of applause to the new Blessed!"

Father Amorth saw the underlying cause of evil in many modern events, including the Italian mafia. In recent times, another significant beatification occurred, this one involving a young magistrate killed by the mafia. What can be more demonic than the mafia? Men (and women) who come together to organize skillfully, only to commit evil: to kill, steal, terrorize, blackmail, and cause despair. On Sunday, May 9, 2021, again Cardinal Semeraro, this time in Agrigento, Sicily, proclaimed someone Blessed. Rosario Livatino was murdered on September 21, 1990, while driving to work without his escort. As a judge, Livatino had investigated the mafia too much, and too well, and had to be stopped. So they stopped him forever. He got out of his car and fled into the countryside. They gave chase, and after he fell, they shot him. He asked, "What have I done to you?"

Before becoming a judge, Rosario Livatino was a good Christian. He always signed the pages of his agenda with a peculiar acronym: STD. Only after his death would its meaning be discovered: *Sub Tutela Dei* (under the protection of God). He placed his life in the hands of God. He used to say that at the end of our lives, we will not be asked if we have been believers, but if we have been believable.

Thus, another modern martyr was beatified. While meeting Livatino's parents in a historic visit to Sicily on May 9, 1993, Pope John Paul II referred to him as a man of "justice and faith." In the Valley of the Temples of Agrigento, this man's life shouted out to the mafia: "The judgment of God will come just once!" What could have been inside the hearts of the butchers of Blessed Livatino and the other so-called "men of honor" if not the hellish action of the devil? How could the human mind, in and of itself, plan and execute the massacre of [terrorist attacks conducted by Sicilian mafia] Capaci or Via D'Amelio in Palermo, or Via dei Georgofili in Florence? Or how could anyone cause a child to die of privation and then dissolve his body in acid, guilty only of being the son of a *pentito* [someone who was informer for the government against the mafia], as happened to little Giuseppe Di Matteo?

What can be behind so many other horrendous stories that have been circulating in the media for years, if not decades? Father Amorth recalled two such emblematic stories. The first involves Emanuela Orlandi, the fifteen-year-old daughter of an employee of the Vatican Prefecture of the Papal Household. She disappeared without a trace on June 22, 1983 after attending music school at the church of Sant'Apollinare. When she left, an eyewitness said he saw her get into a black car. From that moment, nothing is known about her. Pope John Paul II launched an appeal for her release. Every possible lead was followed, but nothing was discovered other than misleading information, lies, and reticence. Who kidnapped Emanuela? What happened to her? Still today, there is no answer. Her family members and brother insist on more information from the Vatican, but they say everything has already been said. Father Amorth offered his opinion:

> I do not believe that a fifteen-year-old girl would get into a car if she did not know the person well who asked her to get in. I believe that it is necessary to investigate inside the Vatican and not outside, or at least investigate the people who knew Emanuela. In my opinion, only someone Emanuela knew well could have persuaded her to get into a car. Often satanic sects operate in this way: they lead a girl to get into a car and then she disappears. The game is unfortunately easy. They get their prey into the car, sedate her with a syringe, and then they do with her whatever they want. Let it be clear that I hope this is not what happened. I hope that if it really is a Satanic sect, as I believe it is, that this sect has nothing to do with the Vatican. I hope this never-ending story ends soon. But I do not shy away from saying that young women often disappear in this way all over the world. Can a girl disappear so close to a place that should be

as holy as the Vatican is? Unfortunately, yes. Because Satan is everywhere.[142]

Father Amorth recalls a second episode which took place in Novi Ligure (province of Alessandria) on February 21, 2001. A sixteen-year-old girl, Erika De Nardo, together with her boyfriend, killed her mother and her eleven-year-old little brother. They stabbed them to death without a reason, without a second thought, and (without a doubt) in an act of unspeakable cruelty. She also planned to kill her father, but he didn't come back home until later and so was saved. What or who could have armed the hand of a daughter, a sister, to commit such a heinous crime? The two were discovered, convicted, and served their sentences. They were eventually released profoundly changed. Erika spent time in the Exodus community run by Fr. Antonio Mazzi. During the entirety of her journey of ascent from hell, her father, whom she had wanted to kill, stood beside her. He helped her rebuild her life.

Father Amorth posed questions and offered an answer: "Can there be any more perfidy in the world than this? More hatred? More anger? It seems difficult to imagine. This is inhuman perfidy. It is the perfidy of the devil."[143] It is difficult to say he is wrong. When the human soul descends into the dark canyon of evil, it can only have been led there by evil itself, which has a specific name: Satan.

How many souls occupied by the devil did Father Amorth encounter? It is difficult to count them because in his thirty years of tiring, patient struggle were countless encounters with the devil. The struggle for the liberation

---

[142]   Amorth, 191–92.
[143]   Amorth, 93.

of humanity from the power of the devil, in which he spent much of his life, was ultimately an apostolate of hope. His was a formidable and terrible battle, with no holds barred. He knew well that Satan openly aims to take possession of humanity, of all people, to snatch them from God. The exorcist stands between his frightening plan and its realization. It is an unpleasant role, not for everyone. Father Amorth accepted and endured it for a large part of his life without ever deserting or giving up. Who knows how many souls he snatched from the devil's clutches.

14

A MAN IN A CASSOCK

Elisabetta Fezzi knew Father Amorth well. She co-authored with him "*Padre Amorth: la mia battaglia con Dio contro Satana*" (Fr. Amorth: My Battle with God against Satan).[144] Her work reveals the interior life of this remarkable Renaissance man, taking her reader beyond his public role as priest, exorcist, and the Pauline. She writes:

> In our first meeting, Don Gabriele told me about his meeting with Don Alberione and how he entered [the Society of] St. Paul without knowing about the Pauline charism, only to follow the *Primo Maestro*, as Alberione is affectionately referred to by his sons and daughters.
>
> My encounter with Don Gabriele began with a simple appointment for an interview, and it could have ended there. But I sensed this was not enough. I

---

[144] Gabriele Amorth and Eliabetta Fezzi, *Padre Amorth: la mia battaglia con Dio contro Satana* (Edizioni San Paolo, 2017).

immediately discerned his fatherly attitude and was fascinated by him. I felt it was necessary to meet subsequently, and we did so for years. As time passed, our talks became more profound, and he gave me a huge gift: that of allowing me to go beyond the person and experience a veritable encounter with him, the man.

It was not easy, because Don Amorth, a true Pauline, knew what he wanted to communicate and how to do so. He had no time to waste, and he did not go beyond the canons that his role, as the most famous and powerful exorcist in the world, imposed on him. Only rarely did he allow anything of himself to surface.

My first thought was about his enthusiasm: Don Gabriele dedicated himself to what was entrusted to him with his entire being, with complete dedication. He was like this since childhood, and he demonstrated it passionately in every assignment he took on: from the spiritual assistance of the Pauline Family groups, to editor-in-chief of *Madre di Dio*, through the consecration of Italy to the Immaculate Heart of Mary.

Every now and then I try to imagine how he must have felt when Cardinal Poletti gave him the mandate as exorcist to help Fr. Candido Amantini, the famous Passionist of the Holy Stairs, who already had the odor of sanctity in life.

It was 1986, and Don Gabriele was about sixty years old. He had been a priest for thirty-two and had not been formed, like most consecrated priests of then and today, for this ministry.

According to the chronicles, at that time there were only about twenty exorcists in all of Italy. The bishops didn't want to hear about exorcisms, much less the priests. It was considered stuff from the Middle Ages. His Pauline confreres were annoyed just thinking about it, as it had nothing to do with the charism of their congregation. The people of God were not well-formed, and recourse to sorcery, as well as the use of other potentially dangerous practices, were rampant.

Don Gabriele made an effort to gather information and learn from his teacher, Father Candido. But he immediately understood that it was not enough to learn the *craft*; the subject was so critical and urgent, he had to go beyond it.

Thus, he put his communication skills to work enthusiastically and founded an association of exorcists. He also worked to arouse the interest of the media who responded to his requests with equal enthusiasm.

He was a real "stage animal," if I can borrow the term, with a strong sense of timing and rhythm. He always wore a cassock, and he showed a great stage presence even when he said uncomfortable and unpopular things with great clarity and determination.

He was a man in a cassock, truly incredible. He was a man in a cassock at a time when the Paulines had already closed him in the attic among the cobwebs. He was tall, bald, with crooked teeth and a welcoming smile, attentive and smiling eyes, and a manner of speaking that was simple and immediate, but profound and striking.

He liked to say, "The habit does not make the monk; rather, the habit tells everyone right away that one is a monk." His manner of speech did not let anyone off the hook, and he knew how to be brutal when he wanted to, also because he had an explosive temper (with due respect), and his rigidity and impatience emerged strongly when things did not go exactly as he said. Sometimes he would ask Rosa and Cristina [his collaborators] if he had been excessive in scolding someone. Then, when he had been too harsh, he would make a call and apologize.

He quickly became famous as an exorcist while he was a Mariologist [*mariuolo*] and not a thief [*mariuolo*], as he jokingly clarified.

And becoming famous changed his life.

He was desperately sought after by half the world of afflicted people looking for help in a somewhat tone-deaf Church in these matters. He was highly sought after by the media looking for interviews, possibly material that was controversial.

How many interviews did he give between 1986 and 2016? We can only guess, because he did not keep diaries or notes. His prodigious memory allowed him to recall everything without needing to keep a calendar. He only had a notebook for necessary telephone numbers.

I often wondered how he did not get bored giving all these interviews. In the end, the questions he was asked were more or less always the same: Are you not afraid? How is it possible that these things happen? How do you know if there are issues [of possession]? Are they dangerous or are they psychiatric problems? How do you keep on guard?

To these questions, Don Gabriele—a man of faith who spent thirty years denying himself—answered with the same enthusiasm, clarity, and simplicity without the slightest sign of impatience to exactly the same questions. It was as if each time were the first time. In fact, we can truly glimpse an aspect of his holiness of life precisely in this fidelity to his ministry.

He was famous. He was a character. He was a challenging character.

He was challenging from the time of his entrance into St. Paul, as he was not a boy, but an adult. He entered after graduating with a law degree; after serving in the military with the Partisans, for which he earned a medal of valor; and after his work alongside noted political personages, such as Dossetti, Fanfani, Lazzati, La Pira, and Andreotti.

The fact that he was so esteemed by Don Alberione was not enough to alleviate a certain mistrust his confreres felt toward him, a mistrust that worsened when he was appointed provincial delegate in 1977.

The founder had died in 1971 and Don Tonni, then superior general, had plans he wanted to put into action. For this reason, he preferred to appoint an executor rather than have a provincial superior elected democratically in the chapter meeting.

Unfortunately, Don Gabriele had no experience as a superior and had not been trained for the post. He was probably not suited to the task and never received instructions from Don Tonni. Thus, that year he aroused strong opposition among his confreres who considered him an intruder. He was too rigid for some, and others believed his ideas were excessively innovative, even revolutionary. His strong character and strict concept of obedience (he held that the order of a superior was the will of God) did not help him in community relations. Paradoxically, the fact that he tried to be friendly was not considered a gesture of friendship but a show of superiority, as if he harbored a certain contempt for his brothers.

The climate of distrust persisted until his death. Indeed, during his long term as an exorcist, it only increased. The constant coming and going of people and the disturbances caused by the afflicted he received were annoying. His notoriety was probably also bothersome. It was calculated that the majority of the house porter's time, perhaps half, at Via Alessandro Severo in Rome, where he lived, was spent sorting mail, receiving phone calls, and scheduling visits all for Don Gabriele. People called and showed up without appointments, and it was up to the house porter to turn away the many obstinate guests.

All this contributed to Father Amorth's isolation. He was very much alone, especially after the people closest to him—such as Don Alberione, Padre Candido, Don Stefano Lamera, and Sister Erminia Brunetti—returned to the Father's house. Among the Paulines, he had only one assiduous collaborator, Brother Pietro Francesco Rossi, who supported him for years until the end of his ministry. In the end, even Father Stanislao, the Passionist who was his right-hand man for years and who is considered his spiritual son, could not be close to him, because he was transferred to another region. Once, I asked Don Gabriele about his loneliness. He replied that he had Jesus, Mary, and his guardian angel, and was never alone. This was an unexceptional answer, we might say politically correct, given by an extremely reserved man so careful in his private life and feelings. He rarely allowed his true struggles to come through.

I believe that, humanly speaking, he was very isolated, though he would never have admitted this to anyone. Even in solitude, his abandonment to the will of God as his useless instrument sustained and preserved him.

Certainly, his assignment as an exorcist contributed to making him challenging even outside his community.

He kept his ministry—which he viewed and lived as a work of charity—close to his heart. He gave of himself totally and tirelessly to this charity and performed exorcisms every day as long as his health permitted. He said things that were truly unthinkable, if not unpopular. Once, in particular, he created a stir when he said: "Bishops who do not provide [exorcists] for a serious case [of possession] are in mortal sin." Then he added, with disarming simplicity: "I do not know what I can say stronger than this." What was at the foundation of such a harsh statement was precisely charity, wanting to ensure that the afflicted could find consolation.

On the other hand, he was an expert in civil and canon law. Thus, when he fired a shot, he measured his words with extreme precision in order to communicate what he wanted to say in a surefire way. The problem was that the media often misconstrued or superficially changed his statements. They were more interested in headlines than content.

His faithful assistant, Rosa, said that about twenty sites where he did exorcisms had to be changed because they were causing problems or trepidation. Rosa also said that people, once healed, would disappear without a trace. This caused him much suffering. Not knowing anything about those he had accompanied, sometimes for years, pained him as he sought an encounter between his own humanity and that of the other.

Being always at the center of attention in such a way could have led him to a feeling of pride. Instead, this was foreign to him. "I'm not worth anything," he always said. "I'm not worth a nickel. I have never had any successes; it is the Lord who has done everything. The Lord has had successes." He did not make such statements for external effect; he was deeply convinced of it. He was the most unabashedly humble person I have ever met. He did not deny that he had done great things; rather, he simply attributed the credit to the Lord or to Mary. In one of our conversations, he called himself proud and claimed that he had no merits, other than the acknowledgment of having none. He considered himself a useless instrument and did not budge from there.[145]

Elisabetta Fezzi tried to count the number of battles Father Amorth had in thirty years of ministry:

There are those who say he did forty thousand exorcisms, some seventy thousand in his lifetime. Numbers are a waste, and you could use them to play the lottery. Always with the same humility, without applying anything of himself, he began the blessing

145   Author's interview with Elisabetta Fezzi, 2019.

by praying the ritual in Latin—without introducing anything of himself. He listened to the stories of the afflicted and surely had an idea of the specific problem he was about to face. However, he did not utilize particular approaches but proceeded with the general ritual of the Church. It was the same ritual and the same prayer, always in an atmosphere of order. Of course, there were extraordinary manifestations of the enemy. But even in the most bitter battles, Don Gabriele never witnessed anything indecorous, such as is portrayed in certain films. He had the utmost respect for the person suffering, who was not a case to be studied but a person—the very face of the suffering Christ. Here, too, emerges his sensitivity as a communicator: he always exalted the work of God and diminished that of the devil by refraining from recounting any "special effects" that occurred during the ritual.

He had adopted a method, suggested by Sister Hermia, which allowed him to speed up the ritual by reducing it to a half hour of prayer. In this way, he was able to see more people, albeit for shorter periods. Experience taught him the excellent effectiveness of this method, which he applied with determination.

He had a great respect for the spiritually sick. Even when he understood that the problem was only psychological, he still gave the blessings, as he considered them necessary. If the person had nothing at all, he shortened the prayer a little and made it clear that exorcisms were not needed. He also received those who did not have spiritual problems, despite being so overburdened with requests because, in his words, "I cannot say no." He was too good, perhaps a little naïve. He trusted people and, unfortunately, many took advantage of his good faith, starting with the many, too many, who still define themselves today as his spiritual children. Then there are his "close friends"—those who had a photograph taken with him, which they spread in the media to get "street credibility." Then there were those who asked him for money, exaggerating non-existing needs. He gave whatever he had.

It was always the same prayer, as I was saying. Can you imagine [repeating] it forty or seventy thousand times? It was always the same, identical, such that he no longer needed to read it, because he knew it by memory, in total obedience to the precepts of the Church.

Thus, in a circular manner, we have returned to the great theme of obedience. For Don Gabriele, the will of the Church, the will of his superiors, was the will of God. Without gloss.

He referred to himself as a Mariologist. He made Mary physically present when he spoke. I had the impression of being able to see her materialize by his side to support and protect him so that the things he dedicated himself to with so much commitment could be fulfilled. He recounted that he never experienced consequences or vendettas from the devil, who, on more than one occasion, told him that "that Woman" was protecting him—almost as an insurance policy! The devotion was mutual. He never let go of his rosary. His closest friends said that even during the final hours of his life, when he was unconscious, he did not release it from his hand.[146]

---

146 Author's interview with Elisabetta Fezzi, 2019.

How is it possible that an ordinary man, a normal man, without particular physical and spiritual characteristics, could go face-to-face with the devil and his hosts so many times and for so long? What is the secret of such a strenuous, exhausting battle? Elisabetta Fezzi continues:

> I believe it was his prayer life, which was foremost whenever he began. He also had a lively sense of humor that allowed him to strike a good balance. How else could he reconcile the intense encounters he experienced during exorcisms with being a religious like everyone else? He did so by telling jokes. He knew many, and he told them with great enthusiasm whenever he could. Self-abasement, quips, jokes, wit, and cheerfulness chased away the evil one, who prefers a sad and worried atmosphere. When he wasn't jesting and being witty, he sang. He had a beautiful voice and sang mainly Marian songs.
>
> In addition to singing and telling jokes, he had a passion for gelato. He liked chocolate. His assiduous collaborators, Rosa and Cristina, brought it to him. They spoiled him a lot, and he shamelessly loved being spoiled.
>
> Precisely because of his joyful nature, the atmosphere surrounding Don Gabriele was cheerful in every situation. At the end of the sessions, he always tried to dismiss the person with a smile, because he wanted to sow hope. I witnessed some of his exorcisms, and I happened to see people who had had strong reactions and had recovered a little while being cordially dismissed with a little pat on the head: "*Piffete, paffete, puffete*" [a nonsensical alliteration]. What he was really saying was: "You are a person and not a

wretched, disfigured, devastated creature, and I, too,
am a person, not a war machine."

And then he would immediately say: "Next! The
next one! Whose turn is it! Come on in, *scugnizzo /
scugnizza*" [a jesting, like Neapolitan dialect for male
or female "street urchin"]. These invitations were the
prelude to the next battle.

Time was precious, and appointments followed
one another according to a strict schedule. The thirty
minutes scheduled for each appointment never went
over even by one minute. He had an uncanny punctu-
ality on every occasion, and his well-known rigidity
expressed itself bitterly when someone arrived late.[147]

In his long life, Father Amorth did more than just clash
with the devil. He shared his days with men and women
saints, official and otherwise, and with important and significant figures of the Church of his era. They offered him
friendship, affection, and support. Elisabetta Fezzi added:

> Earlier I mentioned Blessed Don Alberione and the
> venerable Father Amantini, as well as Don Lamera
> and Sister Brunetti, whose causes for canonization
> have not yet begun, but who lived and died in the
> fame of sanctity. I must also say that Don Gabri-
> ele was a spiritual son of Padre Pio of Pietrelcina,
> whom he visited for something like twenty-six years.
> He knew Mother Teresa of Calcutta well and met
> repeatedly with Pope John Paul II. He worked side-
> by-side and was a friend of Venerable Joseph Lazzati.
> In Modena, he met Saint Bakhita and was a family

---

147   Author's interview with Elisabetta Fezzi, 2019.

friend of the Servant of God Mother Nina (Marianna Saltini, founder of the Daughters of St. Francis). On the day of Don Gabriele's ordination, she was present. I do not know if he also met Don Zeno Saltini, whose canonization process is open, but it is likely.

I wonder if frequenting all these saints does not suggest something also about Don Gabriele's own holiness. Is it possible that they were only fortuitous encounters? Would he have frequented them so assiduously and for such a long time if the Lord had not also shaped his life, like theirs, for his greater glory? Do the saints recognize each other? The answer seems obvious to me.

There is no doubt that the afflicted who knew Father Amorth also considered him a saint. This was evident when his body was exposed after his death at his funeral and the people of God surrounded him with affection and paid him a massive tribute. There was no longer any searching for the exorcist; there were recommendations to the intercession of a saint.[148]

In the final days of his life, he carried the cross of his suffering with Christian faith and resignation. Thus, he revealed another face of his, hitherto unknown but equally convincing, in addition to that of the journalist, the Mariologist, and the exorcist. He demonstrated the sick man, weak and frail, totally and completely resigned to the hands of God, to treatment, to his closest companions, friends, and his Pauline brothers and sisters. Fezzi recounts his last days:

---

[148] Author's interview with Elisabetta Fezzi, 2019.

In his illness, he was serene and resigned to every-thing. He did not get angry, despite the increasingly debilitating infections and hospital visits. He accepted everything to the end without ever complaining. In the final days, when he was admitted to Santa Lucia hospital, he could no longer speak, though he was present and alert. One day, he got the attention of Cristina with his hand and pointed to a spot in the room, though there was nothing. He kept pointing, so Rosa asked him, "Don Amorth, do you see Jesus?" He nodded yes.

Don Gabriele always said that whoever has (these types of spiritual) gifts must keep them hidden. It is possible that he did have them, but in his great reserva-tion, he did not talk about them. This is quite evident to those who assisted him for years during exorcisms. At times, he talked about things and events that he could not have known. He would say things like, "You have to push away that friend who is always around you because she is negative." Or: "When that person calls, you should hang up immediately, you mustn't talk to him." These particular statements appear as lights of the Holy Spirit, but we will hardly know any-thing more about them since he did not leave diaries or notes, nor did he tell anyone about them.

It is a real shame not to have any of these writings. They would be priceless and could help us to better understand the man, his life, and his spirituality. I remember asking him to write a spiritual testament, to which he responded that he would consider it. I thought he forgot about it, because he didn't answer me for a few weeks. It would have been strange if he had forgotten—as he never forgot anything. But by then, he was getting old and sometimes he missed a few beats. Then, out of the blue, he wrote me a letter, strictly by hand as he usually did, telling me that he felt he had nothing to add to what he had already told me about himself and what he had written in his numerous books and preached in his frequent homilies. Regarding humility: Don Gabriele did not know what to put in a spiritual testament, as he believed he had nothing to leave to posterity. It seems to me that this is a message of disarming clarity, which deserves careful reflection.

We mustn't hide it; he was an extraordinary man. If he hadn't left politics to enter St. Paul's, he could have taken the place of [Giulio] Andreotti. If Don Alberione had not stopped him, he could have been nominated for a post in the Vatican, perhaps a bishop. If there had been no hitches, he could have become the spiritual assistant at Cattolica [the prestigious university in Milan]. He could have been successful in any human, professional, or pastoral enterprise he chose.

Instead, he remained a simple Pauline, a great Pauline. He became an exorcist, a great exorcist. He became the father of so many suffering people rejected by all, a great father. He maintained his humanity. He loved God, his creatures, and life. And I knew him.[149]

Many who did not know him consider him *only* an exorcist, albeit a famous one. But he was much more, as is evident from this portrait of someone who spent time with him, followed him, and listened to him. He was a man

---

[149]   Author's interview with Elisabetta Fezzi, 2019.

of many charisms and could have held positions of prestige and power in the Church. But he let God, his Mother, and his guardian angel do everything. He remained a simple and humble priest, the number one enemy of the devil, and the friend of saints. Until the end, he remained on the most exposed trench of the faith, there where the struggle to snatch souls away takes place, the frontier of good and evil, where salvation is on this side, eternal perdition beyond. He prevented so many souls from finishing forever in the hands of the devil and bringing them back to the loving embrace of God. Trusting only in Him and in His Mother: *Sub tuum praesidium confugimus, sancta Dei Genitrix* (Under your mantle we find safe refuge, holy Mother of God). Never were words more true. Never was a prayer more authentically sincere.

15

A VERY STUBBORN MAN, A GREAT JOKER

Father Gino Valeretto was a Pauline priest. He was close to him in his final years right up to the end. He spoke about Father Amorth:

I met Don Amorth when I entered St. Paul and am one of the few Paulines who was taught exorcism by him. In fact, during my liturgical studies, I specifically asked to be able to assist him. Later, I was superior of the community in which he lived in the final years of his life.

Don Amorth was part of the "panorama" of this house, as he lived here for so many years. Since the moment he arrived in Rome, he never left. I always thought of him as bald. Only when I saw photos of his ordination did I realize he once had a tuft of hair. He was unrecognizable!

I met him when I was practically a kid. When I became superior the first time, renovations were underway on the wing where his room was located.

The wing was known as "a hundred cells" because of the small windows. On that occasion, he told me that he had never moved from that room, that he had been there for fifty years. They were small rooms, but with a private bathroom and a space for a small library. There was space for just four rows of books. He told me that his criterion was that for every book that he acquired, one had to leave, so there was a large turnover and he kept very little. It was a good exercise to keep only the important things. He was not fond of objects anyway, and he threw them away.

When he died, he owned very little. Towards the end, he had been giving everything away. I also saw his filing cabinet, which contained only a skimpy folder. In that are the limits of reconstructing his life story.

He was very reserved and had a terrific memory, so he didn't feel the need to write anything down. There is almost nothing written in his hand. When he was sick and not well, I sent him to the hospital for a couple of days for tests. He asked me to call someone he was supposed to see the next day. I saw that there were three people in his agenda book with the same name and no surname. He told me which number to call. He was ninety years old and about to enter the hospital! This is the degree of his memory and lucidity in his final days. He was very determined, but also very paternal. In recent years, he had become like a grandfather who was tender to his grandchildren.[150]

---

[150]   Author's interview with Fr. Gino Valletto, 2019.

While living with him, Father Valeretto became familiar with his most intimate and heartfelt human traits, beyond the public persona. He had strengths and defects like everyone else: knowledge and limits, great faith, detachment from material things, absolute seriousness on questions of faith, a frankness typical of his native region of Emilia, sympathy, and disarming humor. He was a strong man, in sum, who clashed with Satan for thirty years without ever being beaten or defeated by him. Father Valeretto added:

> He was always joking, except for his final year when he held back more and had given up his gusto for strong, pointed quips. Then there was when he reproached bishops who had not appointed exorcists, which some believed was out of line. We talked about it. He explained to me that his reproach was tailored: no bishop could have reproved him, because there is a specific norm in canon law that requires the appointment of a head of the liturgical office, an exorcist, and other figures. Thus, bishops who did not do so were in violation of the norms. As a great communicator, he said it in a lighthearted way, but the issue was very serious and very pointed.
>
> Besides this, you always have to distinguish between what he actually said and what he was said to have said. He didn't talk about certain things: they would nudge him and provoke him, but he just said what he wanted to and that was it. He was the consummate journalist, neither ingenuous nor inexperienced. He was very good at speaking, and he measured his words and the context, adapting his preaching to the environment he was in. We mustn't

forget that he had a legal background, even if he was
not a lawyer—in that he hadn't taken the state exam.
And as a priest, he studied canon law, so he knew
law well.

During the last few years, he had some difficulty
staying up to date. For example, we had to inform
him of changes in canon law: to give public interviews, a religious was now supposed to notify his
provincial superior, or the bishop if he were a diocesan priest. He was used to speaking freely. At least
once a month, he hosted television reporters from
all over the world. Unfortunately, few provided [us
with] the recordings. This is a lost patrimony. He had
a perfect voice for the media—unmistakable timbre,
clear words. This also explains the extraordinary
success he had at Radio Maria.

He was not only precise but also pragmatic in his
statements, at times lapidary. In the end, he lost a lot
of hearing. When it was time to adjust the hearing
aid he used, especially for telephone calls at Radio
Maria, by raising the volume, he resisted: "I do exorcisms and the devil screams, I do not need to turn up
the sound."

There are exorcists who have particular gifts, and
it is easier for them to understand what is happening
within the afflicted. Don Amorth had no such special gifts, although his experience was impressive.
But we must not forget the grace of state: he was an
exorcist, and the Lord gave him the necessary gifts,
also because he took his ministry very seriously. So
he certainly received grace from the Lord for his
work—a fact which, however, cannot be technically
considered a charism.

But in the final years, even if he denied it, I personally observed something more. I recall an exorcism in which someone from the German-speaking region of Switzerland was present, accompanied by a priest. During the prayer, Don Gabriele pronounced the name of a demon whom he usually never called. He either recognized certain symptoms due to his vast experiences, or else he had a type of inspiration. In my opinion, he had [inspirations]. In the final days of his illness, many of those present claim that he saw Jesus and the Virgin Mary. It is certain that he told someone by gesturing that he saw something, but what he saw no one knows. This was only in the end, however. Previously, he never let things slip out. I pried often, but despite the fact that he trusted me, he didn't open up.

He had very few friendships. It is difficult to say which were authentic and which were those people interested in him. I assisted him when he was already elderly, and I can say that he no longer had lifelong friends at that point. He maintained strong relationships with his companions from ordination onward, and on anniversaries he sent everyone good wishes. In fact, everyone called themselves his friend, but I think the only person he really trusted was Rosa. He was a companion to everyone, but friendship is something else. After all, a certain isolation is also normal with his type of assignment.

A couple of months before his admission to the hospital, I went to the provincial to talk about him. Many people were making references to him, even without being authorized to speak or write in his name. There were those who pretended to be his close friend without actually being one. It is well-known that people of all kinds show up around famous people. Unfortunately, Don Gabriele was very naïve, and he would oblige whoever asked him for a letter of introduction. In this way, he appeared to approve certain people he had nothing to do with and who took full advantage of him. In his naivety, he trusted people greatly, even while knowing he was being used. He figured: "I trust you. If you betray me, I'll take it back." The problem is that he didn't always have time to discover the betrayal.[151]

Did Father Amorth leave any successors? He was, it can be said, a sort of founder, or re-founder, of exorcism in Italy and beyond. In short, he was a leader who left a void upon his death. Father Valeretto answers:

No, there is no successor. It would be like saying that he was Father Candido's [successor], but that is not correct. Concretely speaking, yes, because Father Candido passed the sick to him, but they were two very different people who acted differently. Suffice it to say that Father Candido's rule was: "Say nothing to the press, zero. Everything the Church says is enough." But Don Amorth was exactly the opposite.

He was exemplary in obedience. Despite the freedom he enjoyed due to his many responsibilities, he managed his time and travel while respecting his superior, though he was accountable only to the provincial and to the general. He maintained his

---

151   Author's interview with Fr. Gino Valletto, 2019.

independence even in old age. Sometimes it was up to me to call him back to the order, very delicately.

It was not easy to keep him in the infirmary, accustomed as he was to his freedom. In the final years, he had to be lifted up and placed in bed. He was not allowed to get in bed alone, because he had fallen several times and required long periods of recovery. He said, "I understand that I cannot do otherwise, that I have to play a good game with a bad hand. When they put me on my feet, I do what I want; when they put me to bed, I obey and do what they want." But he would get impatient in going to bed early. He considered it wasted time, especially on Saturdays, or when he had a meeting or appointment. He would go out with orders to return at a certain time, which he almost never respected. We scolded him because we had to do so, knowing that when he was busy, he would stop at nothing. When he was reprimanded, he was very calm and impassive. He was very a stubborn man, and was never discouraged at all. Even when he received medical treatment, he did not give up on his commitments. It was an endless struggle. As his superior, I had to reign him in and limit him, though I knew full well that it wasn't possible. Also because stopping him completely would have meant killing him.

I remember the last reprimand as his superior. One weekend, two nuns went to see him. Don Gabriele was a little reluctant, as he said he would not do exorcisms in the infirmary. But they insisted. So he began his prayers and the young nun threw herself on the ground screaming. He immediately stopped, but the other sick priests were obviously fazed. I had to scold him, but I knew it wasn't up to him. He always said to me: "Today being a superior is very difficult." He personally experienced a great shock when he was provincial delegate.[152]

In the Pauline world, which has as its charism of communication and spreading the Gospel through the most modern media, an exorcist could appear—and certainly did appear—out of place, a sort of foreign body that ended up there by chance. However, coexistence never ceased, and Father Amorth certainly never considered leaving his religious family, connected as he was to the *Primo Maestro*, Father Alberione. Father Valeretto continued:

> No superior ever prohibited him from becoming an exorcist, despite the fact that there was plenty of displeasure among us over this appointment. On the other hand, neither he nor the superiors had any idea what would come about due to his assignment, having no experience with exorcisms. But it quickly became an issue. A torrent of people wanted to see him, and as rigid as he was, he received people only by appointment. It was always the same: when word got out that he was in the hospital, some fifty people showed up in the ward on the first day. To protect him, we had to seal him off. Notwithstanding, he never allowed the disapproval of the community to stop him: "You say what you want, I'm going ahead."
>
> At the beginning of his priesthood, he knew nothing about exorcisms. On the contrary, he did not believe in them at all. In fact, since he was very

---

[152]   Author's interview with Fr. Gino Valletto, 2019.

honest, he admitted to anyone who asked him: "Previously, I did not pay attention to these things, I really did not believe in them." He was, of course, familiar with theology, which speaks explicitly of the devil, but he was a bit skeptical, like everyone else. For the magazine *Madre di Dio*, he once interviewed Father Candido. After seeing him in action, he became interested in and passionate about the ministry and began to closely follow the exorcisms at the Holy Stairs. Cardinal Poletti appointed him almost clandestinely, without registering him at the curia. For ten years, he was an exorcist without officially being one, even if it was never a problem because everyone knew he had been appointed by Poletti.

In those years, Fr. Gian Battista Perego, the provincial of the Paulines, had a serious problem: the magazine, *Madre di Dio*, had become a shield of Medjugorje. This led to negative reactions from the bishops, who were against giving too much space to apparitions not yet recognized by the Church. In the absence, however, of any official pronouncements to the contrary, Don Gabriele decided to go ahead. So the bishops asked Don Perego for his head. At that time, he had already begun dedicating himself seriously to exorcisms, and the magazine suffered because of it. Thus, Don Perego had to call him and ask him to choose: the magazine with less Medjugorje or exorcisms. Don Amorth told me that he chose exorcisms also for the fact that he was not willing to give up on Medjugorje. In this way, Don Perego accepted his decision, but asked him to regularize his position at the curia, also so as to receive the salary due to those who have formal positions. Thus, he was officially registered on the list of exorcists. Once again, as always, he obeyed his Pauline superiors.

At times, he could seem superficial due to his jesting. He wasn't at all. He was very careful in his manner of speaking. He was truly exceptional with those who were sick: "Those who come to me are scared and disoriented, so I needn't further frighten them, but encourage them by being witty and joking." It made them feel welcomed and reassured. It was in his character, as confirmed by the old *Annunziatine* who often told me about his jokes. He would say, "cuckoo," to tone things down, not because he was dismissive of their problems, but precisely so as not to increase their fear.

During exorcisms, he charged ahead like a train. The devil tried to make him waste time with wit, jokes, and questions. But he never stopped. [The devil] could say anything and Father Amorth went on undeterred.

I remember once the devil told him, "I'm going to destroy you."

He stopped and asked very calmly: "Well, why don't you do so?"

"Because that Woman protects you."

"Oh, really?" he answered. And he continued with the prayer unperturbed, as if the devil's response was the most obvious thing in the world. That he was protected by Our Lady was practically a dogma, it was obvious.

Although he did not boast about it, he always kept in his room the medal he received for military valor as a Partisan. He always said with great simplicity: "I heard bullets whizzing by me. Our Lady must have protected me, because I don't know how I got out of there alive." He believed it was a miracle.

He was also very regular in prayer, and this made the difference. During those periods, no one could disturb him for any reason. Certainly, he was always very devoted to the Rosary. Even in the end, when we went to see him and we were chatting, at a certain point he raised his hand with the rosary, which he always held in his hand, and he had to start praying. He never made excuses. He died with his rosary in hand. He did not leave it for a moment, not even when he was no longer conscious. It's difficult to say if he knew he was holding it or if it was an automatic gesture. But he never let it go.[153]

He was a man of prayer, as well as of action. He was capable of recharging the batteries of his spirit by isolating himself in colloquies with God and in the Marian prayer *par excellence*: the Rosary of *Paters, Aves,* and *Glorias,* repeated a thousand times, with the same faith as the first time. Prayer was the fuel of Father Amorth's actions against the devil and his plots. Who knows how much all the prayers of that stubborn, pugnacious man irritated Satan. Who knows how much the devil wanted to make him pay for all those souls torn from his clutches. Father Valeretto added:

As far as I know, Don Gabriele had no trouble with the devil. But there is no doubt the devil wanted to make him pay, due to all the trouble he gave him. In the end, I believe he had some difficulties. In fact, he

---

153   Author's interview with Fr. Gino Valletto, 2019.

asked me to recite an ancient prayer for him in Latin, which has now disappeared from the ritual blessing. It is the leave of the soul, a *de facto* exorcism that drives the enemy away. More frequently than we think, the devil comes to tempt when death approaches.

I think that the most beautiful text to read on this subject is found in the breviary for [the feast of] Saint Martin of Tours, which reads, "What are you doing here, bloody beast? You will find nothing in me, wretch!?" In the spiritual tradition, we speak of death as agony, the final agony, which technically is the battle: and the last battle is the one with Satan. According to medieval spirituality, it is the devil who comes to try us at the final moment, at the end of life. I have had the opportunity to accompany confreres who clearly endured the final assault with the devil. With others, I could only guess. For some saints, it is said that their final moments are calm and peaceful, in the vision of beatific things. But on the other hand, there can also be a victorious final attack.

I saw no signs of particular attacks in Don Gabriele, but he was in the hospital. Even though I went to see him every day, I only met with him briefly, so I cannot say what was happening to him the rest of the day or at night. Sick people are usually left alone at night, so if anything happened to him, no one knows. However, I did not notice any signs of overwhelming fear, as he was always very calm. Asking for a prayer is like saying: "I'm sick, give me some medicine." He kept saying over and over that he would aid all exorcists from heaven, interceding for them. I can state that after his death, the devil reacted angrily upon invoking his name.

At any rate, even if I do not know what he was going through, he asked me for the prayer, and I had to look for the Latin text at home. He also wanted another one, but I could not understand which one he was referring to, also for the fact that it was in Latin, a language with which he was greatly familiar, like all those of his generation, as opposed to me and mine.[154]

---

[154] Author's interview with Fr. Gino Valletto, 2019.

16

SAINTS FOR FRIENDS

Father Gabriele Amorth died in Rome on September 16, 2016 after having been sick since 2010. He was ninety-one years old. He had spent sixty-nine years in the Pauline order, sixty-two as a priest, and thirty as an exorcist. He lived a long, full life, rightly—on the side of God.

He took literally the words of Saint Paul, the apostle of the Gentiles, whom Father Alberione chose to be the father and patron of his religious family. With Saint Paul, Father Amorth can proclaim that he "fought the good fight" (2 Tm 4:7). This is not an understatement. He fought daily, and not against a virtual enemy. No, he fought against Satan himself and all his demons. What's more, he took Jesus at His word when He ordered His disciples to cast out demons (Mk 16:17; Lk 9:2). Once he went to this front line, he never ceased battling for souls. He never deserted his station. Many owe him both their gratitude and salvation. Priests, bishops, and popes cannot overlook his example and lesson. Rather, they should treasure them. All of us, probably, will have to recognize evil, call it

by name, face it, and fight it. Satan exists, and many have
faced and continue to face him.

Fr. Gabriele Amorth was a holy man. The Church, one
day, will have to investigate his virtues. Father Valeretto
gives insight into the hidden holiness and sanctity or
Rome's exorcist:

> Some wonder why we buried him in the Laurentian
> Cemetery [in Rome] and not here close to Don Albe-
> rione, in the Generalate of the Paulines [in Rome]. The
> first answer is due to the norms in force, which would
> have required permission from the vicariate and the
> civil authorities. The second is that we preferred not
> to differentiate between other confreres and those
> for whom the cause of beatification will soon begin.
> But if someday it were useful or necessary, we'll see.
> Those who knew him already consider him a saint.
>
> I love him and I knew him, but holiness is a gift
> from God, beyond what we think. There are people
> of exceptional holiness, who, however, do not become
> saints with a date on the calendar. And there are
> others, perhaps less exemplary, who are recognized
> as such by the Church, because the Lord has His
> designs. In Cinisello Balsamo, there is the body of
> Blessed Carino [Pietro of Balsamo], who killed Saint
> Peter [of Verona] in the forests of Concorezzo, then
> converted, became a Dominican friar, and became
> Blessed even though he was a murderer, because the
> Lord willed it so. We must be careful when talking
> about holiness, because we use human tools, which
> are always limited.
>
> Our memory is short, partial. Let's say, for
> example, that Pope John Paul II traveled more than

any other pope. This is not true. Proportionally, Paul VI made more trips in relation to the time he lived, though with less attention from the press. Similarly, we say that Don Amorth is the most famous Pauline in the world. But if we compare his fame to that of Don Alberione and consider the two different ministries and the absence of television at the time of the *Primo Maestro*, we see that the statement is not so correct. Still, on the subject of holiness seen with the eyes of God, we Paulines must follow priorities. In my opinion, there are other candidates for sainthood before Don Gabriele, such as Don Dragone and Sister Erminia, a great mystic, who was very close to Don Amorth.

Holiness occurs when God intervenes directly, and His gift prevails over the natural dimension. In Don Alberione, however great the gift was and despite how he tried to hide it, the human dimension and individual effort were very evident. On the other hand, in Don Dragone, Don Lamera, and Sister Erminia, the divine intervention was superior to the human aspect. Don Amorth is more like Don Alberione. [I say this] not to diminish his holiness but to clarify the different varieties. The fact that Don Gabriele had such close connections with so many saints is cause for reflection. Not recognizing this means not wanting to see the signs and designs of God.[155]

Many who knew him believe that Father Amorth is a saint, including certainly all those he freed from Satan. This is referred to as the "fame of sanctity." It is the sincere

---

[155]   Author's interview with Fr. Gino Valletto, 2019.

belief of those who have been personally touched by the human and spiritual greatness of someone and remained fascinated, struck, and affected by him or her. This has taken place—and still happens, God willing—in many cases, including recently. And it will continue to happen, because God will certainly never allow the Church and the world to be lacking in saints. On the other hand, there is the canonization process; that is, the official and definitive recognition of the holiness of a person after a long, meticulous, and intricate canonical process. Father Valeretto further explained:

> Once upon a time, it was necessary to wait forty years after death to be able to begin the recognition of a saint. The long period was needed to reduce the emotional impact and allow the really important things to emerge. Five years is sufficient today. In the past, the fame of sanctity counted more, and witnesses were secondary, also because after forty years it was not so easy to find them still living. In fact, there are many saints who remained blocked for this reason. Now the canonical process relies much more on witnesses.
>
> Regarding Don Gabriele, he will have to be investigated thoroughly, because he was not only an exorcist. Don Alberione entrusted him with very sensitive tasks, which he carried out with total dedication, as the *Annunziatine* and the *Gabriellini* can testify. Maybe not everyone is interested, but if our founder trusted him so much, he must have had good reasons. There was a very strong bond between them—a very close and affectionate relationship. Don Gabriele had very touching memories of him. For example, between 1959 and 1970, the two saw each other every

two or three days. They made the spiritual exercises together in Ariccia at least until 1969. In the end, the founder could no longer walk, and he was frail and thin. Don Gabriele would take him in his arms and move him from place to place. Before setting him down, he would give him a gentle kiss on his forehead in an expression of tremendous intimacy, tenderness, and trust. I don't know how many other brothers would have dared be so intimate with Don Alberione, an old-fashioned man from Piemonte with a sharp, rather diffident and authoritarian personality. Not that Don Amorth was ever spared from getting a reprimand, but there were indeed strong, tender affections. The trust and esteem were mutual.

He did not leave a spiritual testament, because he didn't think he was going to die so soon. We had him hospitalized merely for tests, and no one imagined it was the end. Despite the fact that he was ninety-one years old, he was still extraordinarily active, to the degree that his strength permitted. He had pneumonia *ab ingestis*, which means there was a faulty functioning of the epiglottis, in which particles of food or drink end up in the lungs where they decompose and cause perennial inflammation. In his case, it caused a continuous cough. He was hospitalized so they could understand how to deal with the problem, perhaps some kind of throat therapy to help him swallow better. So he went to the hospital for a couple of days, as these were the agreements with the doctors. But then it became a week. Later, he had his first intestinal infection from which he recovered, albeit somewhat debilitated. Then he had two subsequent lung infections, and he still recovered.

So we moved him to Santa Lucia because he needed continual care, twenty-four hours a day, which we could not provide at home. Later, he had two serious respiratory emergencies, but was saved by a resuscitator. So we decided to transfer him to Gemini, where they did everything possible. But by then, he was so weak he couldn't hang on anymore. It's difficult to say how aware he was the last few days. He could no longer speak, because his throat was very sore. The last words I heard him say were, "I love you." Then he was intubated, and he lived for a few more hours until his great heart could no longer hold out.[156]

---

[156]   Author's interview with Fr. Gino Valletto, 2019.

17

INHERITANCE

The funeral took place on September 19, 2016 in the church of the Pauline Generalate on Via Alessandro Severo in Rome—the great Regina Apostolorum sanctuary, desired by Father Alberione. It was marked by a large crowd of sobbing people, dozens of priests at the altar, and heartfelt tears. Father Stefano Stimamiglio, general secretary of the Society of Saint Paul, gave the farewell homily.

> Today, we do not wish to mourn your passing. This is not what you would have wanted. Instead, to play things down as was your style, you would say to us, "My brother and sister companions, why the funereal atmosphere? Jesus does not take delight in this! Celebrate! Because I have finally met my Lord. This is a celebration. And what a celebration!"
> We think of you immersed in the love of God—the God you faithfully served as a priest since your ordination way back in 1954—whom you sought since

childhood. But while searching for Him, you always served Him—even when you felt called as a young man to defend the Italian people, our homeland, as a Partisan, at the risk of your life. Yes, because as the apostle Paul says, the Christian, the man of God, the pastor is willing to risk his life and even lose it for his brother. For he knows he has nothing to lose, because he has gained everything in Christ. That is everything. You, as a good Pauline, knew this well and lived it.

And yet you served the Lord even when you were involved in politics, at the age of just over twenty, following in the footsteps of your father, Mario. You glimpsed the shining face of the Lord in the men of God and in the saints you met as a young man: those engaged in politics (the Servants of God Giorgio La Pira and Alcide De Gasperi, the Venerable Giuseppe Lazzati and Giuseppe Dossetti); those consecrated to God in the Church: Saint John Paul II, Saint Pio of Pietrelcina, Blessed Giacomo Alberione, Venerable Mamma Nina, mother of your dear Pauline friend Don Franco Testi, Don Zeno of Nomadelfia; and who knows how many others.

For many years, since 1985, you encountered the face of the Lord Jesus above all in the eyes and faces marked by the suffering of a class of afflicted people whom Jesus loved: the demonized, those troubled by afflictions of the spirit, the doubters, and psychiatric patients who knocked on your door by the thousands in search of help and comfort. They, too, are the *anawim*—the poor of Israel—whom Jesus looked on with compassion, loving and freeing them. You continued doing so for many years through your work as an exorcist of the Diocese of Rome.

Today, a great void has opened up before us. But biblical history teaches us that when every great man of God dies, he leaves a legacy to be reaped . . . And your heirs, dear Don Gabriele, are all of us.

We Paulines and all members of the Pauline family have inherited from you the love for the one whom we call the *Primo Maestro*, that is, Blessed Don Alberione, our founder. You knew intimately his spiritual strength, holiness, and the love he had for Jesus, the Divine Master.

From you who have been a father to many, we priests have inherited a sense of paternity. In a world that is losing its identity, that leads to becoming self-referential and ever more autonomous, without time and space, without a memory of the past or hope for the future, being a father is a sign of prophecy. You were a father to many. You taught us that fatherhood means to be compassionate, to help, to admonish, to give hope for the future, to encourage, and to communicate with gestures and words that we are all children of the one Father who, in the Son, saved us. To be father, you taught us, means to love.

To your many exorcist associates, you have left your experience, your counsel, and your comfort in a passionate, but difficult, tiring, hidden, and important ministry—one that is not always understood and appreciated. For them, you were a teacher, an example of a soldier in the fight against Satan equipped only with the weapons of the Spirit, as the apostle Paul recalls: the loins girded in truth, the breastplate of righteousness, the feet shod in readiness to proclaim the message of the Gospel of peace, the shield of faith with which to quench the flaming arrows of the evil one, the helmet of salvation, the sword of the Holy Spirit, which is the Word of God [cf. Eph 6:14–17]. We thank you because due to your books, interviews, and insistence at every opportune (and otherwise!) occasion, the number of exorcists in the Church increased, even if it not to the degree you would have liked. Due to your being a Pauline communicator, so many exorcist brother priests have been able to train in such a difficult and delicate field. We ask you to protect them and encourage them from heaven so that they may persevere in this valuable service on behalf of the people of God. We also ask you to assist their many lay helpers (colleagues of Rosa, your right-hand assistant for many years), who heroically give their time to this work of spiritual mercy.

Your tormented friends have inherited from you a sense of Christian hope. . . God makes all things new, and He makes our life new. Anyone who has experienced deliverance from the nefarious effects of the devil has experienced this firsthand. Those who are still on the journey know that the enemy of man, the devil, will never have the final word. They also know well that he cannot try us beyond our strength . . . Only Christ the Lord has the final word: it is the cross that saves: *Ecce crux Domini*, Behold the cross of the Lord, we read in the exorcism ritual. The cross does not mean death, but life. This is the ultimate meaning of Christian hope. This is the meaning of the Christian revolution you lived in your flesh.

The people of God have inherited many things from you. First of all, is the spirit of the Beatitudes . . . Poverty of spirit (not feeling grandiose), meekness, thirst for justice, mercy, purity of heart, being peacemakers, being persecuted or afflicted or insulted. To the world, these things are madness; they are the foolishness of the cross. But to those who are being saved, they are the power of God. Discovering peace and joy in suffering, even in diabolical possession, to experience life within death: this is the challenge of the Christian that you, Don Gabriele, accepted, lived, and suffered in your many endeavors among us.

The community of the faithful has also inherited the tragic sense of sin—which our culture challenges or ridicules—and the memory of the judgment on our life that each of us will experience before God on the last day. You fought long and hard against the devil, dear Don Gabriele—that is, against the extraordinary manifestations of Satan. But you never ceased to warn us of the greatest danger that threatens everyone—the most ordinary and, one can say, banal manifestation of evil: that is sin, becoming the murderers of our brothers, of our sisters in the infinite ways in which this is possible.

The people of God have inherited, in sum, your love for Mary. You who witnessed the construction of this sanctuary of ours, the fulfillment of the vow made by Don Alberione to the Queen of Apostles during the war: if no Pauline brother or sister were to die, he would build a sanctuary for her. You, too, were part of this vow, dear Don Gabriele, when you obtained from Don Alberione, during a private conversation with him, (at just seventeen years old) the safe return with your loved ones. You and your brothers were saved and your mother (along with you too) always believed it was her, our Celestial Mother, the Queen of Apostles, who protected you. The weapon of the Rosary is powerful: this is the meaning of your latest book.

Thank you, Don Gabriele, for the person you were . . . And one day, on the last day, when all our tears are dried, we will surely meet you again, a saint among the saints, and you shall say to us: "Welcome, my brother and sister companions!"

The devil can no longer do anything to Fr. Gabriele Amorth. The battle is over, the soldier is safe. He is in the home—and in the embrace—of God.

18

EXORCISTS TODAY

Father Amorth did not live to see the effects of COVID-19, the coronavirus pandemic that struck between 2020 and 2021, and creating an increase of fear and anxiety around the world. He did, however, gives words which may help us see these events more clearly. The devil does not just afflict individuals, he once wrote, but also classrooms, communities, groups, and even society at large. The "effect of Satan's influence on groups," he warned, "is one of the most destructive and powerful." This stems from the effects of psychological woundedness, fear, and lack of faith in the public life. Fr. Paolo Carlin, spiritual heir of the dean of exorcists of Fr. Gabriele Amorth, in an interview with *Vatican Insider*, agrees. "Much can be attributed to the evil one," he said, especially when "one does not see causes and solutions to one's ills." Exorcists who, notes Father Carlin, "number about 600 in the world, of which about 350 are in Italy . . . [must] understand how to help the suffering person who comes to him, also with the help of those in the medical profession."

Father Carlin is the councilor and spokesperson of the International Association of Exorcists. A few years ago, he published a veritable instruction manual, titled *On the Care for the Obsessed: Recognizing Cases of Diabolical Possession, Intervening and Accompanying People with Spiritual Problems.*[157] In it, he explains what it means to be an exorcist today in a post-pandemic world:

> It means being a priest authorized by the bishop (no one else can perform exorcisms) to exercise the ministry of deliverance and healing from the extraordinary action of the devil, which manifests itself in obsession, vexation, possession, and infestation. The ordinary action of the devil, that is temptation, is fought with the tools Jesus gave us: diligent listening to the Gospel—to overcome deceptions, doubts, and fears, and to learn the criteria for making important decisions; constant prayer—to combat the temptation to disobey God; sacraments—to fortify the soul and spirit with humility that is obtained in the sacrament of Reconciliation (confession) and the spiritual strength through the Eucharist, the living presence of Jesus risen and victorious over evil. Sometimes, for various reasons, the intervention of the faith and prayer of the Church is also required. This is expressed in the service of the exorcist priest who, in the name of Jesus and in communion with the Church, commands the devil to leave. Every diocese in the world has one or more exorcists. Many are members of the International Association of Exorcists, which

---

[157] Carlin, *De cura obsessis. Riconoscere i casi di possessione diabolica, intervenire e accompagnare le persone con problemi spirituali.* Used here with permisison.

promotes initial and ongoing formation in the sensitive ministry of exorcism.

Once again, the devil. But hasn't it been said that he
does not exist? Do we in the twenty-first century still have
to deal with this anachronistic, outdated, medieval figure
today in our modern era of the triumph of technology?
Isn't this absurd? Father Carlin responded to this mentality with direct words which echo his spiritual father,
Gabriele Amorth:

> The devil manifests himself in two types of actions.
> The first is the ordinary action of temptation. This is
> the most dangerous, because it is masked by desires
> and plans. It leads one away from the command-
> ments and respect for one's neighbor. Then there is
> the extraordinary action. This is rarer. It occurs only
> after serious sins, such as denying God or engaging
> in the occult and sorcery, but also due to persistent
> grave sins from which one does not repent. Its con-
> crete manifestation takes place in events or situations
> that cannot be explained scientifically, rationally, or
> humanly. In the first [ordinary] case, one falls into
> disobedience to God and contempt for one's neigh-
> bor. In the second [extraordinary] case, there are
> obsessions (in the mind), vexations (marks, cuts,
> bruises, or writings on the body), and even possession
> (this is rarer, with loss of control of the body, which
> is overtaken by the devil). It is said that those who do
> not believe in the existence of the devil do not even
> believe either in God. So they are not Christians, but
> something else. What is certain is that believing or
> not believing does not change reality, which in part

comes from God and is, therefore, good, and in part
from the devil and, therefore, is evil. Whoever says
that good and evil do not exist is a deceiver who
denies reality.

The Church, however, is overly cautious regarding the
presence of the devil, bordering on reticence. It seems, at
times, that instead of keeping the faithful on guard, she
prefers to flatter and adulate them so they'll be good, since
there are so few believers left. Further, the number of
active exorcists is dramatically insufficient for a world of
seven billion inhabitants. Father Carlin's response again
sounds familiar:

> The sign of the presence of the devil is sin in all its
> forms. The Church recognizes diabolical possession
> only in the simultaneous presence of four condi-
> tions: speaking unknown languages, extraordinary
> strength beyond one's physical possibilities, vio-
> lent and uncontrollable aversion to the sacred, and
> knowledge of occult, hidden things. It is impossible
> to know how many people are possessed, as there
> are no statistics. It can only be said that those who
> resort to exorcists are suffering in body and spirit,
> perhaps experiencing Satan's eventual attacks in hid-
> ing, for fear of appearing crazy. In the majority of
> these cases, these are people who have lost spiritual,
> moral, and social points of reference. There are those
> who are obsessed, others vexed, and, more rarely, the
> possessed. There are also cases of local infestations—
> that is, the presence of demons in the form of false
> deceased, noises, odors, of the disappearances and
> appearances of objects.

Now that the pandemic has passed, the devil has not. There is still the need for foot soldiers of God ready to fight—courageous and untiring men, because the struggle continues, and will continue as long as there is only one man left on earth.

Father Amorth continues.

BIBLIOGRAPHY

Among the numerous writings about Fr. Gabriele Amorth, the following books (written by him or about him) were consulted for the writing of this volume.

Amorth, Gabriele. *Angeli e diavoli. Cinquanta domande a un esorcista.* EDB, 2014.

—. *Dio più bello del diavolo. Testamento spirituale.* Edited by by Angelo De Simone Edizioni San Paolo, 2016.

—. *Il diavolo ha paura di me.* Edited by Marcello Stanzione. Edizioni Segni, 2016.

—. *Il mio rosario.* Edizioni San Paolo, 2016.

—. *Maria. Un sì a Dio.* Edizioni San Paolo, 2019.

—. *An Exorcist: More Stories.* San Francisco: Ignatius, 2002.

—. *An Exorcist Tells His Story.* San Francisco: Ignatius, 1999.

—. *Un esercito contro il male. La mia verità su Medjugorje.* Edited by Paolo Rodari and Roberto I. Zanini. BUR Rizzoli, 2019.

—. *Vade retro Satana!* Edizioni San Paolo, 2013.

Amorth, Gabriele, and Elisabetta Fezzi. *La mia battaglia con Dio contro Satana.* Edizioni San Paolo, 2017.

Amorth, Gabriele, and Marcello Lanza. *L'ultima intervista.* EDB, 2017.

Amorth, Gabriele, and Paolo Rodari. *L'ultimo esorcista. La mia battaglia contro Satana.* Edizioni Piemme, 2012.

Amorth, Gabriele, and Stefano Stimamiglio. *Saremo giudicati dall'amore. Il demonio nulla può contro la misericordia di Dio.* Edizioni San Paolo, 2015.

Amorth, Gabriele, and Slawomir H. Sznurkowski. *Ho incontrato Satana. La battaglia del più autorevole esorcista vivente.* Edizioni Piemme, 2016.

————. *Maria e Satan.* Edizioni San Paolo, 2018.

Amorth, Gabriele, and Marco Tosatti. *Inchiesta sul Demonio.* Edizioni Piemme, 2003.

Gaeta, Saverio. *L'eredità segreta di don Amorth. Così la Madonna ha salvato l'Italia.* Edizioni San Paolo, 2019.

Ragona, Fabio Marchese. *Il mio nome è Satana. Storie di esorcismi dal Vaticano a Medjugorje.* Edizioni San Paolo, 2020.